Amora

WHO ON EARTH AM I?

To Angela
Best Wishes
Tery walter

WHO ON EARTH AM I?

Psychic, Alien and Paranormal Experiences

by

Terry Le Riche Walters

Amora

An Amora Paperback

Who On Earth Am I?
Psychic, Alien and Paranormal Experiences

Text and illustrations © Terry Walters 1996
Terry Walters has asserted his right to be identified as author of
the work in accordance with the Copyright, Design and
Patents Act, 1988

First published in the UK in 1997 by Amora
An imprint of Amora International Limited
50 Christchurch Road, Ringwood, Hants. BH24 1DW

Designed and Typeset by Amora International Limited
Printed and bound in Great Britain by
SP Press, Cheddar, Somerset BS27 3EL

A CIP catalogue record for this title is available from
the British Library

ISBN 1 901532 00 3

ACKNOWLEDGEMENTS

Thanks must go to my wife, Dianne for her help in compiling this book and her tolerance of my lifestyle which has become hers also. Times are very exciting and unpredictable, but others can be sad. She shared the early ridicule.

Also thanks to people and friends, especially Sheelagh and Louise for their letters back to me confirming the stories I've written about in this book. It was nice to receive letters from other acquaintances with their appropriate comments.

A special mention has to go to John Harman for his help with the front cover and other illustrations and also to Tracie Mason for her help with the illustration of the male Orion.

A general thank you to everyone who has given me support, from clergy, doctors, medical staff, politicians, show-business people, ufologists, Egyptologists and, of course, my family.

Some names of people mentioned here have been changed to protect their identity.

Terry Walters

WHO ON EARTH AM I?

This is a small part of my lifetime experiences to date consisting of many strange phenomenon, which include alien visitations and telepathic communication with them, to healing, ghost riddance, the stars and Egypt to name but a few.

My experience as an alien contactee is so strong I feel it is different to other peoples accounts of alien contact. The knowledge and messages I receive are overwhelming and at times very concerning.

Many events have been witnessed by friends, family and perfect strangers who can corroborate certain happenings and mysteries. Some stories are in this book.

I feel I derive from Egypt because of my profound awareness of Giza and the pyramids. In this book I will reveal what I saw through my psychic mind when I visited Giza recently, it is quite outstanding.

I hope this book makes compelling reading. It is not meant to upset or shock. I felt I should share my experiences with a view to help others undertand and cope, who are maybe having some similar things happening in their lives.

Terry Walters

PREFACE

As Assistant Editor and Marketing/PR Manager of the magazine 'UFO Reality' I meet many interesting characters and I count myself fortunate that I have spent time with some of the world's leading psychics. Terry Walters is however in a different league. He is the best of the best.

Throughout his adult life Terry has helped countless hundreds, possibly thousands of people with the help of his extra-terrestrial friends from the constellation of Orion.

As a result of working with Terry I have experienced something unusual which my colleague Jim Mills, research editor of the magazine, can corroborate to some degree.

I suffer badly from migraine headaches and had been in bed for two days with one particularly bad attack. 'Grasping at straws' I asked Terry's 'friends' to help me over the appalling pain. When I awoke a couple of hours later about 3 a.m. I opened my eyes and clearly saw the distinct shapes of four people in my room. My mind went blank with astonishment, I simply fixed my gaze on them and as I did so they seemed to dissolve into the night.

The following morning I felt great. Jim had been spending the night in our guest bedroom and when he came down into the kitchen for breakfast I asked how he had slept. He replied, 'Not very well, I could have sworn that something was in my room last night, a presence and it really 'put the wind up me'.

The most striking feature of this book is the weight of evidence, not only circumstantial, but physical as well, supported by the number of credible witnesses who have willingly come forward to testify on Terry's behalf.

Read on and see for yourself!

Mike Ktomi

CONTENTS

LIST OF COLOUR ILLUSTRATIONS

INTRODUCTION

Terry Walters was born in February 1943 in Croydon Road, Penge, South East London. He moved to Bracknell in 1957 and now lives in Wokingham, Berkshire. Terry has three grown-up children and several grandchildren.

Not wanting to expose his children to possible ridicule whilst they were young, Terry has only recently spoken out about his ongoing contact with extra-terrestrials from Orion. Now Terry has chosen to face the sceptics and the detractors, because he knows that what they have to say is of little value.

Terry has written this book because he believes that the story he has to tell and the message he has to give is too important to ignore.

Extra-terrestrials, Egyptology and psychic phenomena: Terry believes that now is the time for the truth to be told, and listened to!

Prepare to be amazed ....

CHAPTER 1

My Early Years

W ho on earth am I? Day by day, I am still trying to piece together the answer.

My birth or shall I say rebirth took place in February 1943. I feel certain I am a reincarnation of an ancient Egyptian Pharaoh, and that I have a connection with the star constellation of Orion. I believe I came from a planet from behind this system.

I have tried for some time to find the right 'ears' in the scientific community, to listen to what I know about this constellation. This has happened only very recently. I have spoken to a number of scientists and astronomers and described how planets have been created from behind Orion.* They were astounded by my accurate insights and said I was absolutely correct. They were also intrigued to know from where I gleaned my data as I am not a scientist.

A ceremony is very vivid to me, in which I know I took part. It happened in Giza at the Pyramids.

I feel the Pyramids are far older than documented.I would put a time of around twenty six and a half thousand years ago. The ceremony I believe I took part in many thousands of years BC was when the stars and the sun were in a particular point in the sky. I was standing with my back to a temple; before me was the Sphinx and beyond that the Pyramids. Suddenly a large red glowing sphere, which I can only call a 'sun-disc', fell out of the sky coming down between the two large Pyramids of Chephren and Cheops. It then rolled down and came right over the top of the

---

*Apparently there are two nebulae, Orion and Horsehead, 'behind' the constellation and these are considered to be the birthplace of new planets.

Sphinx and finally engulfed me with a feeling of mellow-ness, in a place of tranquility. The feeling was that I was in a spirit world.

I believe my life started when I died, which may seem rather bizarre, but let me explain. I remember being on a planet which was at war with another. It was a far superior race. They used very advanced technology and were extremely aggressive. The planet I was living on may have been the Earth; it was not as hostile, and was under attack.

My planet was losing the war and I could see my family dying and I must have been killed myself. The next thing I can remember was the start of this current lifetime; being born in my mother's womb. I could see the water. As strange as it may sound, as my mother was giving birth, I heard conversation and saw three beings standing by me. This was to be the beginning of many unusual events to happen in my life.

All during my childhood my mother said how strange I was and that she was unable to hide anything from me as I had the ability to know what she was thinking. I could also read the minds of other children at school. I used to think they could do the same, but I was not old enough to under-stand that I was different.

In the early part of my childhood I had many contacts with the 'beings', which I now know are definitely 'friends' from beyond Orion. They were not particularly nice to me at first and I can remember being frightened by them. I know that I was abducted several times because when I ask my mother why I had to go into hospital so often, she would shrug it off and say that I hadn't. On one occasion when I was nine years old I tried to get away when the people from Orion appeared. I threw myself down the stairs, breaking my shoulder blade. My mother told me that I was taken to the hospital to get my broken shoulder strapped up, but a couple of days later I took the dressing off and went swim-ming, there wasn't any more pain.

My mother has told me that as a young child I hardly slept. She said she spent many an hour holding my eyelids shut and singing to me. This was because I was very frightened by the visitations.

One vivid event I recall, was when I was with a friend walking along a river bank. Suddenly an Orion person approached me and proceeded to make a small nick in my leg, causing it to bleed. Wondering how I could explain this injury to my parents, I decided to say I had cut it on a bottle.

My friend David, who was with me at that time, has only recently told me that he could remember this incident. He said he saw me in a mist when it occurred. I have tried to glean more information, but David said he 'clams up' and gets scared when he remembers the event; and it makes him frightened of me.

As I got older, I realised that the Orion people (hereafter referred to as the Orions) were in fact my friends, and up to a point, I believe that they are my original family and I actually love them.

The Orions said that in 1992 more folk would start to come clean about their experiences, and there would be many more sightings of UFOs: They said that books would be published with explicit information and there would be much more television coverage on the subject. This has turned out to be correct. Most weeks on the television there is some kind of mention or programme on UFOs, true case stories and abduction.

In 1993 I told my mother that I was going to visit some of my family in London, near to the place where I was born. She said that I should visit an aunt who had also experienced some weird things in her life. I was intrigued and decided to go and see her.

Upon arriving at my aunt's house we soon got talking. She said she suffered with a bad back. Even after treatment it was not improving. So someone had highly recommended a house in Croydon Road, Penge, where psychic healing was done. My aunt said that although she was sceptical, all else had failed and she had decided to give it a try. Apparently she was seen by a healer and, after a couple of weeks, to her surprise her back became much better. She visited the house several times to find out more, and to her amazement, my aunt discovered she had the healing power. My aunt continues to visit this house, but now as a healer. I was extremely interested to learn more about this and I decided to visit the house myself.

Soon after seeing the house in Penge, I discovered that this was where I was born. This pre-war house was strange and with its long garden it appeared to 'stick out' amongst the surrounding new houses and maisonettes.

Apparently the ground upon which the house stands is sacred, and this is the reason why it has not been pulled down. When I asked my mother about this, she was never very forthcoming. If I want to find out about important episodes or events in my life, I always have to 'grill' my mother. Maybe if my father had been alive he would have been able advise and help me more. However, one thing my mother did say was that after I was born we stayed in this house, and some 'not so nice things happened'; there was poltergeist activity - furniture was thrown around the place.

I still have many avenues to investigate to gain a clear and complete history of my birth.

CHAPTER 2

The Wedding and Matthew

M y life was changed in 1979 by a distant relative of my
wife who I met at a family wedding, and to whom I
will be forever grateful. This man, who I shall call Charlie,
gave me the confidence to start confiding in my family and
friends about the many experiences and emotions that I had
being keeping to myself for so long; and come clean about
the fact that the Orions were part of my life. This confidence came after Charlie advised me to start writing and
drawing the words and predictions the Orions told me and
showed me in my mind.

However a lot of the information enters my mind very
quickly, pages and pages of it; so that there is no way I can
write it all down at once, or even make sense of it all. For
instance, on one occasion after telepathically receiving
pages of information, I asked my Orion friends what it all
meant. They told me that when I had worked it out I would
be able to use it. What they were trying to show me was
something extremely useful, 'free-energy', and how to
employ it; so that I could lift up a bus with my little finger
if I chose to!

Returning to Charlie for a moment, he said that an elec-
trifying force came off me, and that I was the most powerful person he had ever met. He continued to tell me a lot
about myself, and said I would probably need him soon. He
left his telephone number just in case.

During our conversation Charlie quizzed me about a
young boy's life I had saved. I was puzzled at first, until he
mentioned the boy's name, Matthew. Then I recalled who
he was talking about. Five months prior to the wedding, a
neighbour's five year old son, Matthew, was playing on a
deep, frozen pond near my house. Though the edges of the

pond were frozen solid, in the middle the ice was thin and Matthew was heading towards it.

People can react strangely in this sort of situation; some builders working nearby for example, told me later that they had seen Matthew in danger, but they had chosen to walk away rather than get involved. I shouted at Matthew to get off the ice, but he was a very defiant child and he took absolutely no notice of me. I urged him again to stop going any further, but he wouldn't get off the pond completely. So I ran to fetch his mother, who sped back with me and managed to retrieve him.

Charlie somehow knew that I had prayed for him and he suggested that I continue doing so as Matthew still needed my help. This confused me: how did Charlie know anything about Matthew and my connection with him? Charlie also said that Matthew would have probably fallen through the ice and died had I not acted so promptly. I began to wonder if it was more than coincidence that I had been on hand to help save Matthew? Had my Orion friends acted as guardian angels? Despite my growing experiences of the extra-terrestrials, I had not considered it before and certainly, on the day of the wedding I remained puzzled as to why I should still need to pray for Matthew.

It wasn't until the summer of 1990 that I found my answer. An old neighbour, Bob, had moved to Gloucester several years earlier, and my wife and I had stayed in contact with them. Consequently, I received an invitation to visit them. Upon arriving at their home I felt a special atmosphere. They told me that they had someone in their lounge who they wanted me to meet. I knew immediately who it was when I saw him - it was Matthew, now a young man.

It turned out that Matthew's family had also moved to Gloucester and lived about four miles away from Bob. Somehow Matthew had discovered that I was visiting them and had arranged to meet me there. When we met, Matthew shook my hand very firmly, started to thank me, and asked what I did for him twice a day. I replied that I prayed for him, as I was asked to. Matthew said he knew this, as he experienced a soothing feeling go through his whole body whenever this happened.

Matthew invited me back to his parent's home. When I met his parents they told me that their son had a heart condition, and somehow Matthew knew that through me he was being protected. By now I had realised that my Orion friends had guided me to the pond that fateful day, many years before and that in response to my prayers they were still looking after Matthew. It seems to be a pattern that once they have helped or spared a life they continue to do so.

Whilst I was chatting to Matthew's parents in their sitting room, I mentioned that in my minds-eye I could see some lovely pictures upstairs in their house. I described the winter scenes and frames that they were in. Matthew's mother looked at me in astonishment and promptly went upstairs and brought them down. They were exactly as I had described. It turned out that Matthew's younger sister had painted them. I think the reason I picked this up was to give her a little boost, as she was very insecure and uncertain of her talent. I told her to pursue her painting and to have confidence. I felt that the Orions were probably part of their entire family now.

The stepfather showed me a family photo which was on their mantle shelf; this led me to tell him about most of his life and family history. He was startled by my accuracy.

I feel that I owe a lot to Charlie, he gave me the confidence to start sharing with people the unusual occurrences that happen in my life, as I did with Matthew's parents. I also know that my Orion friends are with me and encouraging me all the time.

Back Operation

Back in 1966 I was working as an electrician. I had recently married Dianne and was trying to lead, as much as possible, a near to normal life. I know my wife thought I was strange at times but I had told her about myself.

One day after finishing work I was loading some electrical equipment into the boot of my Mini car. The boot was not well designed and I had to lift and load the goods at an awkward angle. As I was doing this I felt a sharp pain shoot through my back; I was in agony and I wondered how I was going to drive home. I did, but by the time I arrived the pain was excruciating. As I was getting some numbness in my legs I went indoors and lay down on my bed. Not being keen on visiting the doctors I thought that with rest the pain might go away, but I was wrong. I finally gave in and saw the doctor who referred me to a Consultant at the local hospital.

A few weeks passed and I was still waiting for my hospital appointment to come. The pain was really starting to get me down by now, so one afternoon I thought about my Orion friends and asked them if they could help me. That evening at approximately nine o'clock I was lying in bed when one of them came and stood next to me. I soon became aware of others; they took me through my bedroom window and down a corridor which led into a spacecraft which was brightly lit in a bluey-white colour. Once on board the ship I was taken through a small honeycomb shaped room leading to a larger one, which I can only describe as being an operating theatre. Telepathically I knew that they wanted me to lay on the table on my stomach. As I did this I unconsciously made eye contact with one Orion.

Looking into his eyes was like looking through the slats in a venetian blind with a very bright white light flickering behind them. Continuing to gaze I became completely paralysed, but remained conscious.

Out of the corner of my eye I saw movement and something that didn't look like any of the Orions with whom I am familiar. The being looked slightly reptilian and, although I couldn't see it very well, I was terrified! I then realised that this creature was performing an operation on my back; it only lasted for a short time and there was no pain. Soon I was back in my own bed and had quickly convinced myself that it was all nothing more than a very bad dream.

In the morning I got out of bed without giving my back pain a second thought. It was as though the pain had been erased from my memory, and I actually went to work.

What is strange is that I never received any appointment from the hospital for X-rays or treatment. My wife and I never spoke about it again. I know this story sounds hard to believe but it is the truth!

After about eighteen months I started to get flash-backs of what had happened. It became obvious that the Orions had carried out an operation on my back. I believe that their intervention has probably prevented me from ending up in a wheelchair.

Several years later, after many encounters, I realised that the operation was a major point in my life. I now had built a lovely bungalow and had a large swimming pool installed.

One summer's day in 1986 I was stooping over the rim of my swimming pool at an awkward angle trying to clean it, when to my horror, I felt a terrible pain in my back. The pain was so bad I had to visit my doctor, who suspected that I had trapped a nerve. He arranged for me to have an X-ray at the local hospital.

Two weeks after the X-ray I was called back by the hospital for several blood tests; they took from me what seemed an excessive amount of blood. When the results arrived I was again recalled to the hospital. A specialist asked me if I would mind meeting some other experts who would like to ask me some questions. I agreed and was led to a conference room where I sat down to answer their queries. There were approximately eighteen people present. I was asked about what I drank and what I ate. For example: Did I drink fizzy drinks? Did I eat beef burgers? I was asked about my sleeping pattern and what exercise I took. I asked the nearest specialist what was wrong with me. He said there was nothing wrong and he commented that he would like to swap bodies with me, even though he was almost half my age.

I was told that I had no rheumatism or arthritis, but I had extra 'things' in my blood. Whatever it was, fought off infection; for example, if I cut myself the wound would heal quickly. They could also not understand why my body was making extra zinc, though this was considered a good thing. What I remember most about the interview was the surprise and shock on the doctors' faces after reading the medical data and examining me.

Now the bombshell came! Where had the operation on my back been done? I knew where, but how could I possibly tell the specialists that?

I just decided to say that I had not had an operation. The doctors' faces turned to surprise and doubt. I was immediately taken to look at the evidence - my X-rays, which were lit up on a wall by a light box. One doctor pointed out the lower part of my back where the surgery had been carried out. He said that an excellent surgeon must have performed the operation on my back due to the extensive damage that had occurred there. The X-rays were contrary to what I had said and clearly the specialist did not believe me. I also felt that the matter would not be left alone, so, at this point I said, 'I am an Alien!'

A week later 1 received a letter from my General Practitioner saying that the hospital had written to him asking where I had the lumbar surgery performed. He wrote back and said that he had checked all my medical records and that I had never been to hospital for back surgery. After this correspondence nothing was ever said about the matter again. Even when I visited the doctors over the next few years with minor ailments, the matter was never spoken about.

In the summer of 1994 I was watching our local television station 'Meridian', when I saw the 1960s pop star Reg Presley, lead singer and writer of the 'Troggs', talking about UFOS, Crop Circles and the Government Cover Up. My ears pricked up as a song Reg had written in the 1960s, had just been re-released by a group called 'Wet Wet Wet'. The song was called 'Love is all around'.

Prior to seeing Reg on the television, the words to that song had been playing on my mind for weeks. At that time I had not heard Wet Wet Wet's version. My son suggested that I tune into the Sunday Chart Show on the radio and hear it being played. This I did and when I heard the words it was like an extra-terrestrial message. I had a huge lump in my throat, it was very emotional. Every sentence in the song means something special to me.

After hearing this song on the radio I asked my 'friends' where the words came from. They told me they wrote it for Reg Presley and that I was to get in touch with him to try and find out what was happening. It wasn't too difficult to find Reg. It appears that when I need information 'out of the blue', the right people always seem to come my way. Though this is done cryptically at times, my 'friends' sort things out.

My daughter Julie was on holiday in Blackpool at this time and she knew I was trying to contact Reg. She rang me on the first day of her holiday and said that she had bumped into someone who knew the Troggs; apparently they had worked for them years ago and had a contact number. Julie of course rang me immediately with it. I rang the number and left a message saying I would like to speak to Reg Presley, and would he kindly return my call. A few days later I was driving my car, when the mobile telephone rang, it was Reg. He introduced himself and asked me what I wanted to know. I asked him why he had written the song 'Love Is All Around'. Reg replied that it had only taken him ten minutes to write, it just came into his head. Reg did say that he was not able to comment too much on the subject, and I respected that. However, we decided we should meet, at a hotel near to his home.

At the meeting was Colin Andrews, author of many Crop Circle books. We swapped some very interesting stories and Reg and Colin were fascinated about my back operation. Reg appeared to be fed up with all the cover ups going on and was prepared to help me. Prior to going back to the hotel, I managed, (with some difficulty) to get the 1986 hospital X-rays of my back surgery. Colin Andrews said that he was leaving for America that evening, since he lived there most of the year. He said that he would like to take the X-rays with him, so he could have them examined by a top American specialist. This way the findings could be independently validated. In due course he would contact me with the results.

Before Colin departed I wanted to ensure that as far as he was concerned, my story was credible. Therefore I told him something I had picked up in his mind. I knew he had been working on a theory that sound emitted by UFOs, as they entered the Earth's atmosphere, was similar to that made by grasshoppers. That is, a frequency just under a microwave. He was astounded and asked me to repeat what I had just said. He switched on his tape recorder and recorded it so that he could play it back to his wife. He then went on to give me more details about what I had just said. It was extremely interesting.

Shortly after this I went to the toilet. On the way back I felt a pain in my right knee, however I knew I was being told that Colin had a painful knee and would have to have surgery. Colin was really shocked when I told him and said that I was right, he did have pain in his knee. He went on to explain that he was going to get it attended to. Colin switched on his tape recorder again and repeated what I had just told him. Then he asked me how I could have known this. I felt good about this happening because it had ensured some sort of credibility. I then placed my hand on Colin's knee, and as I did so Reg's song 'Love Is All Around' played on the hotel radio. We all looked at each other and I said to Colin, 'This is your lucky day'. I felt my 'friends' healing through me, and knew his knee would get better.

Reg rang me after a few weeks to say that he had some good news and could we meet. At the meeting he showed me a letter he had received from Colin Andrews. It was a copy of the findings from my X-rays. They had been examined in one of the best clinics in Connecticut. The findings were quite technical; I had undergone surgery, there was no doubt. The damage from the original injury had shown up on the X-rays along with scarring. It appears that the procedure and surgical precision necessary to fix my back was an impossibility in 1966.

I also received a letter from Colin who told me that after I touched his knee he'd had no further problems with it. I feel very grateful for the help Reg and Colin gave me, they had listened without doubting what I had said.

After further communication with Colin I told him what the specialists had said about my blood results: 'That they were strange'. Colin asked if I could get the 1986 blood test results so that he could get them analysed. I did have quite a problem getting them and tracking the doctors down, who had moved or left the hospital. I eventually got the original blood test results and I sent them to Colin.

As anyone could see, it appeared that the typed set of figures had been altered by someone, going over the original figures with a pen. I can only think that the only reason they were altered was to make them seem ordinary. After reading the comments from the clinic, what is one supposed to think? I am certainly not suffering any illness.

When I speak to people about myself, especially my

CEDAR HOUSE
SURGERY

269A NINE MILE RIDE, FINCHAMPSTEAD, BERKS. RG40 3NS.
Telephone: Eversley (01734) 328966 Fax (01734) 734710

27th August, 1996

TO WHOM IT MAY CONCERN

RE: Terence Walters - d.o.b. 22 2 1943
     Walmer Lodge, NIne Mile Ride, Easthampstead, Wokingham

According to the medical records which are in my possession, Terence Walters has never had an operation on his back.

Yours sincerely,

Dr. R. Latham

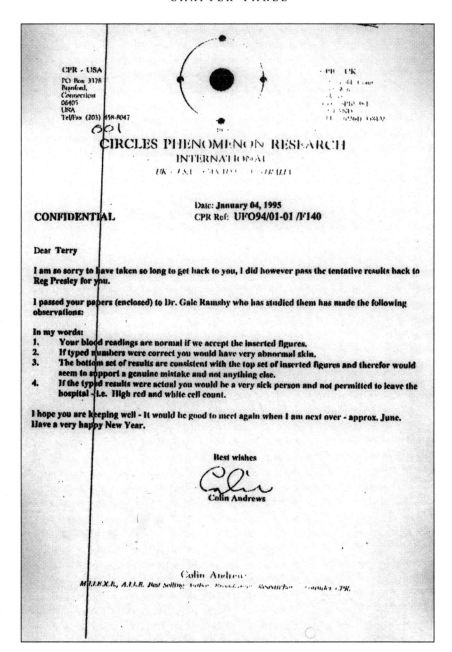

CPR - USA
PO Box 3378
Branford,
Connecticut
06405
USA
Tel/Fax (203) 458-8047

CPR - UK
illegible

CIRCLES PHENOMENON RESEARCH
INTERNATIONAL
UK · USA · CANADA · AUSTRALIA

CONFIDENTIAL

Date: **January 04, 1995**
CPR Ref: **UFO94/01-01 /F140**

Dear Terry

I am so sorry to have taken so long to get back to you, I did however pass the tentative results back to Reg Presley for you.

I passed your papers (enclosed) to Dr. Gale Ramsby who has studied them has made the following observations:

In my words:
1. Your blood readings are normal if we accept the inserted figures.
2. If typed numbers were correct you would have very abnormal skin.
3. The bottom set of results are consistent with the top set of inserted figures and therefor would seem to support a genuine mistake and not anything else.
4. If the typed results were actual you would be a very sick person and not permitted to leave the hospital - i.e. High red and white cell count.

I hope you are keeping well - It would be good to meet again when I am next over - approx. June. Have a very happy New Year.

Best wishes

Colin Andrews

Colin Andrews
M.I.F.X.B., A.I.I.E. Best Selling Author · Broadcaster · Researcher · Founder CPR.

THE UNIVERSITY OF CONNECTICUT HEALTH CENTER

September 12, 1994

Department of Radiology
Farmington, Connecticut 06032

Colin Andrews
C.P.R.
Guilford, CT 06437

Dear Colin,

Thank you for allowing me to examine the radiographic images on Mr. Terance Walters. My understanding is that Mr. Walters suffered an injury to his back following which he has confined to a wheel chair and then at some later time was subjected to some form of procedure which apparently restored his ability to walk in a normal fashion.

The examination consists of copies of three radiographic views, an AP of the lumbar spine, a lateral of the lumbar spine centered at the L2 level, and a cone down lateral centered at the L4 5 disk space.

There are five non rib bearing lumbar segments. The spinal canal is at the lower limits of normal both in the AP and lateral dimensions most narrowed at the L4-5 and L5 S1 levels. In addition there is narrowing of the L4-5 disk space and more marked narrowing almost complete collapse of the L5 S1 disk. This disk space is also surrounded by osteophytic spurs. A small deformity involving the anterior lip of the L5 body might be consistent with the patients history of previous trauma. Degenerative arthritic changes are noted about the posterior articulations of L4-5 and L5 S1 causing further narrowing of the spinal canal and encroachment on the narrow paramotor most marked at the L5 S1 level. Incidental note is made of an area of irregular calcification in the right sacra iliac joint, a finding that most likely has no pathologic significance.

In view of the patient's history there is no evidence for surgical intervention in the usual way of approach to the disk space through the posterior lamina. Further evaluation of this area might better be done by means of computed tomography or magnetic resonance imaging.

Although there is no visible evidence of a surgical intervention this does not rule out what is termed a key hole laminotomy performed by some of the modern neurosurgeons a procedure which is frequently not accompanied by bony changes. In addition, percutaneous diskectomy can be performed in which there are also no definite radiologic changes. Therefore, the possibility of a surgical intervention that is not visible on these studies remains. Aside from this, the significant findings relate to a congenital type of spinal stenosis further compromised by degenerative changes about the posterior articulations and degenerative disk disease at the L4-5 and more severely L5 S1 levels.

If I can be of further assistance in this matter, please feel free to call me.

Sincerely yours,

Gale R. Ramsby, M.D
Professor and Vice Chairman
Department of Radiology
University of Connecticut
School of Medicine

An Equal Opportunity Employer

connections with extra-terrestrials, they ask if I have any proof. I feel sure that these results must count as some sort of validation.

Extra-terrestrials have visited me several times when I have needed medical treatment. Here are two more stories that I would like to share with you, because I believe people are looking for proof and corroboration.

During my early life I did a lot of boxing, I came from a boxing family. This resulted in one of my front teeth being damaged. There came a time when the tooth started to turn black so I visited my dentist. After taking an X-ray of it the dentist showed me the results. The roots were clearly smashed and it was dying, so an appointment was made for an extraction. When I went to have the tooth taken out, the dentist explained that since the roots were broken into frag-ments, he would have to cut into the gum and dig the pieces out - it was a surgical job. However I felt that, if I really concentrated on this tooth, it would be all right and it could be pulled without cutting the gum. So I asked the dentist just to pull it. He said me that it wouldn't help, that he would still have to get the roots out, and showed me the x-ray again. I urged him to try and reluctantly he did. The tooth came out intact, roots and all - like magic. The dentist was amazed and gave me the tooth as a souvenir. I recently contacted this particular dentist and asked if he remem-bered the incident, and if he minded me including this story. He said, 'Terry, I will never forget it, I tell everyone about it'.

As a child I suffered from many ear infections which have resulted in a lot of scar tissue. In the summer of 1995 I went swimming and, unfortunately, some water got into one of my ears. After a few days the ear was aching badly. So I decided to get it checked out at the doctors, where it was suggested that I have both ears syringed. After the nurse had finished this procedure, she checked my ears and noticed something in one of them. She went and fetched the doctor to have a look. Coincidentally, the doctor happened to be an ear nose and throat specialist. He examined my ear and asked me where I'd had the surgery done, since it was a fairly new procedure.

Apparently this particular surgery involves something inside the ear being brought forward for better hearing; I cannot remember the correct term he used. He did say that it was being used for children with glue ear. I thought, here we go again! I told the doctor the operation had been performed on a UFO and I waited for a reaction. He said 'Oh, you have had it done privately and you do not want to say?' and we left it like that. I have not yet probed any further into this matter, who knows what I will discover?

In the summer of 1993 my daughter Angela and her husband moved into a brand new flat on a recently developed housing estate in Binfield, Bracknell. During the eighteen months they lived there, they experienced two strange incidents:

Over a period of time, Angela informed me repeatedly that her bedside clock started talking around dawn for no apparent reason. When I enquired as to what sort of talking clock it was, Angela replied, 'That's the problem, it's simply an ordinary digital clock'. I went around and inspected it and sure enough it was. Angela said it had been doing this for some weeks. She said that when the clock was speaking, she could hear a conversation, although it was not clear enough for her to hear the actual words; it sounded similar to the communications she had heard on televised space flights when Mission Control at Houston spoke to the astronauts. Lee, Angela's husband, was a heavy sleeper and had not heard the clock until one morning, in her frustration, she woke him up to listen when it started to speak. When Lee heard the voices, he instinctively threw the clock out of the window.

The second incident occurred when Angela, Lee, my son Chris and his wife Stephanie were watching television at the

34

flat. Suddenly they witnessed a small round orange coloured object fly pass the window. They were all quite bewildered. The orange object repeated the same performance about a month later. After discussing this incident with me, it all started to make sense. Where I had been taken on board the UFO for my back operation was precisely where Angela's flat had been built. The strangest thing of all is that Angela has a second storey flat and this would have been the precise height of the UFO.

CHAPTER 4

Egypt

E gypt has been the biggest puzzle of my life, I have always wanted to go there and especially see the Pyramids at the Giza plateau.

In May 1995, I received a phone call from a Mr Robert Bauval, co-author of 'The Orion Mystery', apparently he heard about me through a friend. We made a date for him to come to my home and listen to what I had to say about my life, with particular reference to the star system of Orion. As it happened we had to postpone the meeting and arranged one for a week later.

On the new date Robert arrived and I had a very valuable discussion with him. He became very excited when I told him about a ceremony that had taken place thousands of years ago at Giza. I told Robert that this ceremony often recurs in my mind. This is what happens:

I am standing in front of the Sphinx between the two large pyramids, the sun falls down between them, it comes over the front of the Sphinx and engulfs me. I then feel very mellow as if nothing matters or bothers me. I do not know where I am, just in a very strange place. I hear what seems like chanting. I then wake myself up by shaking my head. As I was telling him this he urged me to repeat it all again so that he could tape the conversation for his friend Graham Hancock (co-author of the book 'Keeper of Genesis').

Robert said that he had been investigating this ceremony for the last twelve years. As I have said, originally we had planned to meet a week earlier, but Robert had to cancel. It was during the intervening period that Robert had discovered the explanation to the information I had just given him about the ceremony. Consequently what intrigued Robert, was that if the original meeting had occurred, my story would not have meant so much to him.

The ceremony which I experienced, had, according to Robert, happened thousands of years ago. His own research revealed that an important Pharaoh stood on the spot I had described and the 'sun disc', as he put it, came down and engulfed the King and took him into the spirit world. Robert asked me if I would like to travel with him to Egypt in November 1995, and said he would introduce me to Graham Hancock and John Anthony West. John had discovered that water erosion around the Sphinx indicated that it was much older than previously thought and he had made a documentary about his findings. I took up Robert's invitation and duly went to Egypt with my wife and a friend, David Harvey.

After a good flight we arrived at Cairo airport at 11 p.m. our time, 1 a.m. Egyptian time. We got a taxi to Giza and booked in to our hotel. It wasn't until morning that we realised how close to the Pyramids we were. It was both a breathtaking and deeply moving sight. After breakfast, Robert hired a taxi. Robert was born in Alexandria, and he was able to negotiate a rate because he speaks Arabic. This was clearly a great asset for us.

We visited the Giza Plateau and the Pyramids. We walked around the site and went at first into the Great Pyramid. On entering a very low passageway to the Queen's Chamber, visitors are forced into a crouching position and it gave me the feeling that this was intentional; as if you are made to bow to a 'higher being'. We entered the Queen's Chamber which is made out of limestone, with two shafts in the walls, one on either side opposite each other. One of the other walls had a 'niche', this wall is on the immediate left as you enter. I stood back and through my psychic mind I could see that it took the shape of a large beautifully coloured bird, a phoenix, with fire coming from its head, and it had a very intelligent human mind! I could see that this room was some sort of device to bring the spirits and souls from Orion to Earth. I also felt that behind that same wall, to the top left hand side exists a chamber which is concealing something very important. Perhaps on my next visit I will find out what it is.

We left the Queen's Chamber and entered into the Grand Gallery towards the King's Chamber. About halfway up the Gallery I felt that to the right of the wall which backed on to the Queen's Chamber, there was something sealed in behind the blocks. My wife, friends and I proceeded into the King's Chamber. The noise of other people talking in other parts of the Pyramid made a high-pitched humming sound. I immediately recognised this as the contact sound I receive from the 'beings' from Orion when they send me a telepathic message. One part of the ceiling in the King's Chamber is concave, and I felt that the place was designed to be like a parabola, which picked up signals like microwaves, or some other sort of electrical impulses.

The sarcophagus in the chamber is like the re-entry capsules of the Apollo or shuttle craft which have silicon tiles to stop them burning up on re-entry. The sarcophagus has a granite coating which is designed for the same purpose. I am going to be bold by stating that I believe it came and went through the Pyramid as a transporter of spirits and souls. Books on Egyptology suggest that the sarcophagus was put there whilst the Pyramid was being built, since it was too large to go through the entry door of the chamber. I laid down in the sarcophagus and had the feeling of some pressure being put on me, as if I was being pulled down and pulled up at the same time. I quickly got out of it feeling quite sick.

My theory is that the Pyramids were used as a huge electronic machine which appeared transparent and would glow when 'working'. The sides were brilliant blue and the tops were white. I could see them, as if moving like big jellies. I had no compulsion to enter the other two Pyramids. My intuition told me that the small Pyramid, Mycerinus, is like a power plant, and is the most important one, it sets the other two Pyramids working. I walked around the back of it (northside) and sensed it would be an advantage to anybody who was sick. It had a healing energy coming from it. To sum up my feeling of the Pyramids: they are ancient alien electronic technology, far beyond our intelligence - created for the birthing of Pharaohs - a people making factory! I am doing more psychic research on this and the results will appear in my next book.

After a busy first day in Egypt we decided to have a meal at the hotel restaurant and go to bed. During the night I had the most amazing visions. I told Dianne that I could see a large bird, it had a human face and at the end of its large wings were long fingers. I saw it appear - flying around the top of the Pyramids, it did a full circle around them first and finally landed standing on the largest Pyramid, it faced the other two Pyramids with its arms reaching straight towards them. Then my vision was brought into the present time and I saw fourteen priests some of whom were in the grounds of the hotel. They wore black Egyptian robes, and their head-dress was rather strange. I could see what looked like black beads on them. I felt that they were some sort of high priests of importance.

During the early morning at approximately 6.15 a.m. we had an earth tremor, the whole room shook including the walls. My wife woke me a few minutes into it, at first she thought it must be me shaking (I often do this) but she soon realised it was getting stronger. I said to Dianne as a joke, 'That's it! The Pyramids have taken off, they are all UFOs'. (At the time we didn't know it was a tremor.)

Our friend, David, rang through to our room to tell us of the tremor. David is so interested in what happens to me, and so much was going on in the short time we were in Egypt.

We decided to look out of the window to make sure that the hotel was still intact - it was! We arranged with David to get dressed and meet in the restaurant. We were only there a short time when Robert Bauval came in, he was in a state of shock.

'Terry!' Robert exclaimed. 'Your aliens tried to pull me out of my bed, they got hold of my feet and the whole place shook!' We explained that there had been an earth tremor. He said that two of his books, The Orion Mystery, had fallen on the floor during the tremor and both their titles had partially been covered by other books. The way the books had landed made both titles read - ORION TERY.

Robert said that he believed all that I had been telling him, including that I came from Orion. I told Robert about my experiences in the night including the phoenix and the priests. I think we all felt rather peculiar that morning. We decided to rest for a while longer and then go to visit the Sphinx. Robert turned to go to his room and so did we, but on the way back, he said he had some Egyptian tarot cards and instead we ended up on the terrace of his room looking at these cards. They were placed face down on the table and in turn, David, Robert and I picked one. When we turned the cards over they revealed the Sphinx, the Phoenix (which looked the same as the one I had described in the Queen's Chamber) and a priest - we all felt a little 'spooked'. Robert then proceeded to tell me about the fourteen priests I had seen in my mind that night. He said that I had described the fourteen priests that were in-charge of fourteen temples around the area, which depicted the fourteen parts of Osiris dismembered by his brother Set. Robert said the priests did have beads on their head-dress and were dressed in black. Apparently there was a temple nearby. Soon it was time to go to the Sphinx.

I was extremely excited, this was something I had been waiting to do for over twelve thousand years! To me this was the last time I visited there, so I was anxious to see what memories would come back and what I would now experience.

We arrived at the Sphinx quite early during the morning. Robert's extensive knowledge of the area was very helpful in explaining things to us. There were some excavations taking place in front of the Sphinx, and this area was cordoned off. In my mind I could see that the whole area was a maze of underground tunnels. I saw water running uphill towards the Pyramids! I explained this to Robert, who said that he would try to get permission for both of us to get down to where the excavations were. Robert spoke to the Egyptians who were working there and they invited us down to see the work they were doing. The dig was taking place in a dip in the ground, exposing what looked like a bridge. There we discovered a cracked stone 'drain-like' cover with water running upwards - uphill!

Robert escorted David, Dianne and me inside the temple ruins which are in front of the Sphinx, and there we spent a quiet hour absorbing the atmosphere. Robert said to me that he would talk to the guards and try to get permission for he and I to stand between the paws of the Sphinx. This proved difficult; permission was given by one source but soon cancelled by another. Finally, to my delight, it was agreed and we were given two minutes.

We walked towards the paws of the Sphinx, it was enormous - a breathtaking experience. I felt no stranger to it, on the contrary there was a real affinity. Between the paws of the Sphinx there is a large tablet covered in hieroglyphic writing, which says :

"This is the beginning we come from the Stars".

Robert asked me if I knew what the missing hieroglyph was. I drew him a picture, he said 'Yes, that could well be what it is'.

When I first examined the Sphinx, I initially looked at its face. It didn't seem to mean much. Then all of a sudden I could see it staring back at me. It appeared frightening, the eyes were black and powerful. I felt I could not look into them, but I did. The face seemed to transform into a Red Indian Chief, the whole thing looked bigger, as if it was going to stand up and come to life. I believe I saw how the Sphinx was originally, before the changes. The colours were outstanding. It had a magnificent head-dress, the colours were gold, blue and ebony.

My friends were taking photographs and buying souvenirs from the many tinkers. Meanwhile Dianne and I walked off whilst I told her what I was seeing through my mind. It is hard to put into words and would people believe it if I told them? Apparently when Napoleon arrived at the Pyramids he slept in the King's Chamber all night. When asked what he saw, he also said 'You would not believe me!'. Though it may be difficult to believe and I cannot explain everything; the best I can hope to do is to try and put it into words, so that people will understand what I saw.

To put it briefly I could see that the whole area of the Giza Plateau was a huge base for spacecraft. These craft arrived and departed from the star systems of Orion and Sirius. I could see how it was all those years ago. I told Dianne I could see beings of all different descriptions getting on and off the landed craft, some were of half animal appearance, others looked like dwarfs. They all looked very busy. The craft were enormous. I could see two large vibrating beacons about a mile apart. They were like a homing device for navigation for the craft to land. I stood around just staring and taking in all that I was experiencing - it was completely over-whelming.

Before I went to Egypt, I knew only too well that there was a special place where I could stand, it is a way through to the Spirit World, a sort of gateway. It is some distance away from the front of the Sphinx. Without my companions knowing, I instinctively led them to this spot. As I stood there I went into and through a misty atmosphere, then returned, all in a matter of seconds. I repeated it, the second time for a good ten minutes and whilst this was happening I was still able to talk to my friends. This must sound unbelievable, but it is true - it happened.

After this, everyone was talking about getting some lunch before going to the Cairo Museum. We had lunch Egyptian style, it was most enjoyable, inexpensive and different. Robert Bauval showed us where to go, we ate from the side of the road, from a place similar to our sandwich bars. Joining in the culture was great fun, and no - we didn't get a bad tummy. We were fine all week.

Our taxi was waiting to take us all into Cairo. The taxi was an experience in itself, an old 'clapped out' Peugeot 405 estate. The drivers are absolute maniacs, but they did not seem to lose their temper, and lots of honking of horns went on. It was my first time in a third world country, it was strange to see first hand how most working families lived, little huts with hardly any furniture, just a log fire in the middle and perhaps a television. Sometimes they had their animals in with them! When we were in a traffic jam I looked out of my side window to come face to face with two water buffaloes sitting in the back of a pickup truck. As we neared the centre of Cairo and the traffic got busier, little children were begging all over the place, they were trying to sell boxes of tissue paper. Our taxi drivers always seemed to buy from them, it was their way of distributing wealth to the less fortunate.

Finally we parked at Cairo Museum. Robert walked around with us pointing out many interesting artefacts, explaining the history of Egypt, the Kings, Queens and Pharaohs. We were shown the 'Ben Ben Stone', a capstone which they believe would sit on top of the Pyramid. As we arrived quite late in Cairo, the tour given by Robert was a little rushed and so we decided to go back sometime during the week for another visit.

We neared Giza on our return journey, it was now early evening and we decided to get an Egyptian style take-away.

Then we drove and parked near to the Sphinx. The sun was disappearing quickly, setting down behind some large sand dunes. We raced up a high dune as best we could through the thick sand to watch the sun finally set. We also thought that it would be great to have a picnic up there since it was an excellent advantage point. As we ran, a pack of wild dogs came rushing up, I was a little apprehensive at first, but they were fine, just hungry for our food. We settled down to eat. The view was fantastic. The Pyramids looked so magical and mystical. We sat for a while eating our picnic, soaking up the atmosphere. Then we returned to the hotel and sat in the bar talking to one another about the events of the day. Later we had a proper meal in the restaurant and returned to the bar to reflect and speak on the day's happenings.

We all met around the pool in the morning and decided to visit the Step Pyramids at Saqqara. Once again we had an amazing time. As we crossed part of the desert to go to an underground tomb a fierce sandstorm blew up, we could hardly see where we were going. It was difficult to walk. Robert commented on how weird it was that the whole atmosphere was different whilst I was there. He said that we should make a video of the events, since it was like an adventure from 'Raiders of the Lost Ark'.

When we did manage to reach the tombs with the aid of a guide, we discovered that we had to descend a very long way underground via a spiral staircase. It was like going down a well. When we reached the bottom, there were three burial chambers - the King's Tomb being directly in front of us. We entered it through a narrow low passage. It opened up into a small room which had perfectly preserved hiero-glyphic's all round the walls. Our friend, David, crawled into a faultlessly hollowed-out stone tomb which was in the shape of a body. He was only in there a few seconds when all the lights went out. We found ourselves in pitch darkness. At this precise moment I saw the room turn blue and I felt a hand trying to rip my guts out. I knew I had to get out and

I urged Dianne to come with me. I asked if anyone else wanted to leave but they all appeared to want to stay. The Egyptian guide who was with us lit a match, and as he was dressed all in white, I shouted out 'Blimey it's a Ghost!'.

With this the guide jumped about a foot in the air. I couldn't help laughing. However, I was in pain and wanted to get out. We left with the assistance of the guide who lighted about a hundred matches on our way out. We stayed up top on the desert for about ten minutes and then decided to go back down to see the Queen's and Son's Chamber. We were only down there a short while when the lights came back on. The Queen's Chamber was wonderful, the ceiling was full of stars. When everyone had finished looking around we left. The sand storm was still very strong but we crossed over the desert and went to the Tombs of the Sacred Bulls near Saqqara. We went into an underground tunnel. There were masses of tombs on either side of the corridors that supposedly held the sacred bulls.

The most sacred bulls had a white star upon their foreheads and the Pharaohs travelled the world to find them. These tombs were enormous and, originally, hermetically sealed for the Pharaohs had captured and imprisoned evil in them. But eventually in a search for treasure, greedy men blew open the Tombs releasing the contents into the world, bringing chaos. I think it will take a 'high-being', a Pharaoh, to again subdue evil and return the world to order. After an hour in these magnificent tombs, which were covered in perfectly preserved hieroglyphics, a guide ushered us out.

That evening whilst we were in the bar of the hotel, Graham Hancock (author of 'Fingerprints of the Gods') and his wife arrived. They were spending a few days there. We had previously met them in London. We had a drink and then I proceeded to tell them of the psychic events that had been happening to me whilst I was in Egypt. I mentioned the large bird I had seen landing on the Great Pyramid and other inexplicable things that had happened during my life.

The next morning we met up with them again at breakfast. Graham invited Dianne, David and myself to go to Cairo Museum with them. He said that John Anthony West would be there giving a guided tour to some visitors. We all met up with John, and as we walked around listening to what he had to say, we came across a statue of the bird I had witnessed. Graham exclaimed 'That's the bird you have seen!'

In the museum there was a chariot with some extra pieces laying on the floor beside it. The museum guides told the tourists that they didn't know what they were for. In my mind I went back to the time of the early Pharaohs; I knew the answer and told John Anthony West how they fitted onto the chariot. He said 'You are possibly right'. I could relate to many things in the museum and passed my comments on to our company.

After the tour Graham introduced me to John on a more intimate basis and we decided to have lunch in his hotel in Cairo. I explained to him as much as I could about myself in the short time we had together. John found what I had to say very interesting. Time was getting on, so Dianne, David, Graham, Graham's wife and I, all returned to Giza. That evening John was taking his guests to spend a few hours in the Great Pyramid to meditate. I was invited to join them. I declined because I thought it would not be beneficial to me, and I'd arranged to see the Pyramid 'light show'.

I felt very close to the Egyptian people in the village of Nazlet El Samman, Giza. I knew I was exchanging thoughts with some of them. We instinctively knew what each other was thinking. I felt so much at home sitting in a little bar with them drinking hibiscus tea and playing dominoes.

Graham Hancock's taxi driver took us to the 'light show', he said that he wanted me to meet an Egyptian friend of his. This friend turned out to be very valuable and important to me indeed. We were definitely spiritually 'in tune'. Due to the delicacy of the information we exchanged, I cannot divulge it. One comment he did make to my wife when meeting her for the first time was: 'Hello, you are still very annoyed about Terry selling your car aren't you?' Dianne was very startled but not shocked since she has lived with the paranormal all her married life. I did sell Dianne's beloved car six months prior to our Egyptian visit and, yes, she was still mad about its sale. This Egyptian friend has subsequently given me some very interesting contacts in his country.

After leaving my Egyptian friend's home and the 'light show' I met up again with Robert Bauval, Graham Hancock and John West at another hotel, we had drinks and met another interesting person, a Doctor C. Norton, from New Jersey, USA. This doctor is highly respected in his profession. Since he was a doctor I told him about the different things I had experienced; the operation that had been performed on me by the Orions and their colleagues and the healing that I had given to people. I spoke to him about the unfamiliar medical terms the Orions had used. Doctor Norton knew that the story must have some validity since I described medical procedures and used jargon which only an experienced professional would know.

Dr. Norton, informed me of a strange experience he once had when he had stayed all night alone in the King's Chamber of the Great Pyramid, it was the first time he had ever done this. At first he was all right, but then he felt he was being paralysed from his legs upwards, he had trouble breathing and as he sat up he saw a blue ball of light coming for him out of the wall. Just when he thought he was going to pass out, or possibly die, he felt as though he was being cradled in a woman's arms - like a baby.

I said to Dr. Norton, 'That wasn't a blue light coming to you, it was going from you, it was possibly your spirit and soul going from you. I believe that the woman you felt was the Queen caressing you, she gave you a new life'. The doctor looked at me very emotionally and said, 'You know, that could well be the case, since that incident I've had a much better life and very good luck'.

For the last day or two in Egypt, Dianne, David and I spent some time taking in the sights. We visited Memphis and other significant places in the area. It was very enjoyable and we had great fun with our taxi driver. On the light hearted side of things, I would like to share a tale of an incident that happened on the last day we were at the hotel.

A few years previously I had appeared on a television show in Norwich, to talk on the subject of UFOs. The editor of The Sceptic magazine approached me. He said 'You only come on these shows and speak of aliens and UFOS because you lead a boring life'. He went on to say 'you describe your aliens as Scandinavian tourists'.

Well, back in the hotel in Egypt, Dianne and I were returning to our rooms after supper via the swimming pool, when a tall, blonde haired, blue-eyed young man passed by us walking very swiftly, he said in a broad Norwegian accent 'Hello, I am your neighbour'. Jokingly, I said to Dianne 'Wow! That's my Scandinavian tourist, quick follow him'. When we caught up with him, he was standing near the banking desk in the hotel reception area. Standing beside him was another young man exactly the same - his identical twin. I said 'God! Two aliens!' I asked Dianne to approach one of them and ask where they came from and what they meant by, 'I am your neighbour'. One twin told Dianne 'We are from Norway' - (imagine this in a broad accent) - 'We are in the room next door to yours'. I asked one twin if he had been to the Pyramids that day, he said 'Yes'. I said 'How were they built?' He told me 'They were built by levitation, but not by people from this planet'. Then I noticed that both of them had a large star drawn or etched on the back of their hands. I said 'What is that star for?' One twin said 'We just doodle'. I found that rather interesting. I turned to Dianne and said, 'I'll find out what this is all about'.

By now David had joined us. Moments earlier Dianne had rung through to his room to tell him about the twins, and of course he came over immediately. I explained to David what the editor of The Sceptic magazine had told me, so he could relate the story to the Norwegian guys. We all had a good laugh. I told David that the editor had given me a copy of one of his magazines whilst at the TV Show. David asked if he could see it when we got home. When we did return, I invited David round to my house to swap photos etc. I remembered that he wanted to look at The Sceptic magazine, so I got it for him. David glanced through it, stopping at a particular page, he looked a bit startled and bemused. He showed me what he was looking at. There were two sketches with captions.

In the first sketch was a man with a star drawn or etched on the back of his hand; exactly the same as the twins. He was pointing to it saying:

The New Age Scarification. The Ancient method of getting in touch with ones 'self'.

I found this fascinating, as in a way, I was visiting Giza for this purpose. In the second sketch - the same man was still pointing at the star saying:

I obtained, the concept direct, I think from an Elemental Spirit.

(The word 'elemental' meaning the power of nature, essential, an ingredient, first principles of an art or science, data employed in a calculation.)

Most of the time I was in Giza I was trying to work out the power of nature and elements, free energy etc. I certainly was getting 'data' for want of a better word from the Pyramids, Sphinx and the Orions.

I think my Norwegian tourists were trying to tell me something!

When we eventually left to return to England my Egyptian friend came to our hotel at five in the morning to say good-bye, almost like a lifetime friend would. I was told that apparently some of the Elders of the town of Nazlet had sensed my arrival in Giza. They had said that they did not want me to leave.

On reflection it seemed impossible that the whole Egypt experience, along with the people that I met, was crammed all into one week. It was an unforgettable time. I will be returning soon to Egypt to learn more.

CHAPTER 5

Meeting a Leading U FO Researcher and Making a Television Appearance

A few years ago a gentleman by the name of Omar Fowler asked if he could come to my home and interview me, as he was very interested in things I had previously told him. Omar is a very well respected U FO researcher, and has been investigating the phenomena for approximately twenty six years.

We finally met and started the interview, Omar had his tape recorder running and began listening to what I had to say. I was talking for about five hours answering Omar's questions. The conversation was mainly about the Orions I communicate with, their craft and how they travel. I tried to answer all the questions fully, but it's difficult to put a lifetime of experiences across in one day.

Omar had been listening tentatively during the interview and I remember thinking, 'God, what will he make of all that!'. I sat back and waited for his comments. I was pleased when I saw him look at me reassuringly. Then Omar said he believed me, he could relate to everything that I had told him, and that I must have had 'first hand' knowledge to have described with accuracy what I knew, especially the craft used by the Orions. I think we were both were quite exhausted after all of the talking and decided to call it a day, but we decided to definitely stay in touch.

To this present day I contact Omar either by letter or telephone when I telepathically receive information, especially if it concerns global or complicated scientific matters. The information I pass on usually results in Omar calling me back in a shocked or excited state, informing me that what I had told him has actually happened; or that the 'messages' that I have passed on after some analysis proved to be very important.

Omar's response increased my confidence to open up to others more than ever about what I knew. I feel that UFOS and the extra-terrestrial phenomenon are so important that I cannot understand why there are so many 'cover-ups'. Many intelligent and influential people speak of their encounters, surely they should be taken more seriously? It is with this outlook that a friend, Doreen rang me saying that she had contacted a television studio about me after watching a breakfast programme. Viewers were asked if they believed in UFOS and to ring in if they felt that they had been abducted by one. Doreen said she had rung them on my behalf, and hoped that I didn't mind. Doreen told them about me and some of the things she had personally witnessed. Apparently the television studio was so intrigued that they decided to contact me.

I received a telephone call about mid-afternoon from the studio and was duly invited onto the breakfast programme. After listening to what it was all about I decided to give it a go.

Initially, I had to give a brief account of what I would be talking about. They seemed pleased and I was telephoned again a couple of days later to finalise details. I was a little concerned as to whether I was doing the right thing, going so public on a very popular show; I knew it was a very controversial subject and, I suppose to many people, unbelievable. I also had to come face to face with a researcher and told her personal details about herself, and she was intrigued because we had never met, we were complete strangers. One of the things I revealed to her in the telephone conversation was, that she was going to be very successful in her work.

The morning came for my wife and I to drive to the Anglia Television Studios in Norwich. We arrived about mid-day at the hotel, giving us plenty of time to unwind and adjust. During the evening whilst having dinner in the hotel restaurant I recognised a lady, Jenny Randles, who is a

Ufologist. I had seen her once before, on a television programme, and presumed that she was also here for the next day's show. I had questions I wanted to ask her so I requested her room and telephone number from the receptionist.

I contacted Jenny and explained that I would be appearing on the show, she confirmed that she would be as well. I told Jenny a little about myself. She asked what year I was born in. I replied 1943, Jenny said that some of the things I had told her appear to have happened to other people. She told me that in the early 1940s the Ufologists believed that aliens were experimenting with humans and that I could have been a part of it. I don't know whether there is a connection. I've not journeyed down that path in detail yet.

After breakfast we sat in the hotel lounge to wait for our taxi to take us to the TV studios. We noticed a young married couple sitting nearby, who were also waiting for a taxi. The woman had very heavy make-up on, almost 'clown like', I obviously tried not to stare or say anything. The man appeared to be scrutinising us and he came up and asked me if I was doing the television show. We quickly learned that this couple were UFO sceptics appearing on the same show. The man seemed ready for an argument and said that he was going to prove people like me were wrong. He pulled out a newspaper cutting and said that he had the proof. Even to this day I'm not sure what he was on about. As far as I was concerned he posed no threat to me.

Eventually the taxi arrived. We had to share our cab with two more sceptics, who were very rude to my wife and I. After twenty minutes we arrived at the studios and we were greeted by the researcher who had made the phone calls and arrangements. She said that she knew straight away who I was when I entered the building. We all went to the hospitality suite where food and drinks were laid on. My wife spoke with John Stapleton for a short while, he was hosting the show. The programme took place, I felt the general response was good, and not as negative as I had first thought it would be. In fact some of the sceptics were lost for words. I would go as far as to say that they hadn't researched the subject at any length at all, there was so much they didn't know. (There is more to UFOs than Roswell.)

When the cameras stopped, quite a few of the audience came up to me, many full of questions. I had a lot of support, and listened to some very interesting people and conversations. The presenter and researcher thought that the programme went very well.

I noticed that the couple we had met at breakfast were looking at me. The lady then came up and asked me if the Orions were with me all of the time. I answered 'They can be'. She went on to say that during the programme she couldn't help staring at me, and she had felt a presence leave me and go into her, this had made her feel really strange. The lady explained, that unbeknown to me, she was suffering from shingles, and a rare skin complaint that caused her to 'blotch'. It was for this reason that she applied heavy make-up. She had thought that the heat from the studio lights would cause her face to go completely red and 'bumpy'. 'But look at me', she said, 'it's all gone!'

Her husband looked shocked, first he stared at his wife and then at me. He said her shingles marks were disappearing as well as her discomfort. I had to agree, her face looked completely different from how it had been earlier, her skin appeared normal.

They wanted to stay and were asking questions about me. I was very hot and tired and just said that what happens to me is real, it is the truth. I suggested that they ought to take the time to find out more about people like me, who experience strange phenomenon - we are not all 'nut-cases'. This lady, I believe, was very lucky, something did take place, I am certain. It seemed like my 'friends' were saying, 'Yes, we are here!'

My wife and I returned to the hospitality suite for some

more refreshments whilst we waited for our taxi to return us to the hotel. A researcher came up to me and said that the phone had already started to ring, and that people wanted to talk to me. She said that she would contact me over the next few days with the messages they received.

We started our journey home wondering what our friends and neighbours would be thinking, especially those who had no idea about this secret part of my life, let alone the things I had revealed. Both of us were anxious to get home, as we had left a neighbour looking after our dog.

When we got home the first thing my wife, Dianne did, was to make a fuss of our German Shepherd and take him out for a walk. I remember thinking that she had been gone for a long time. When Dianne got back she said that it had taken her an hour to walk just a short distance, as neighbours who had watched the show were curious to find out more and had come out of their homes, bombarding her with questions. The neighbours were asking her what I was like, and the main questions were about the 'healings' side of me. She said that I never professed to be a 'healer', it just seemed that whenever very sick people were around me they appeared to get better.

One of my neighbours who we vaguely knew said that they needed to speak to me. They were extremely interested in what I had been saying on the television. I felt that I would like to see them, as I had been told previously by a relative of theirs that the family were very spiritual and a bit psychic. I walked down to their house and spoke to them for a long time. A few members of their family needed some medical help for different problems. One of their daughters, who I will call Jill, was quite poorly, she is diabetic and was particularly low. I felt that she needed help, as well as this, the family had other difficulties. I picked up many feelings from them. I didn't promise any 'miracles', but hoped things would improve for them.

They were interested in the Orions I described, and

thankfully treated it seriously. I predicted that they would be getting a solicitor's letter in a few days, which duly arrived. They said that they had a spirit guide aged ninety years, apparently she had told them that they would be meeting me. I visited Jill over a period of about a month and she got very much better. I knew she was being helped by my 'friends'. Jill became very involved in what was happening to her, she told me that she had felt things changing inside her body.

One day while I was out Jill came to my home in a panic; she told me that during the evening she had written two pages of 'automatic handwriting'. She had tried all morning to contact me but thought that perhaps I was out for the day, so in a dilemma she took the handwriting to our local library to try and decipher it. Jill said that she was so amazed at the way she had written it, as it was so neat and precise, quite unlike her usual untidy handwriting. The local library could not help or understand it, at first they thought it may have been Hebrew, but it wasn't. They told her to go to the bigger library in Wokingham, this she did. Jill said that by this time she was very uptight and hoped that I was back home. Wokingham library couldn't help her either. However, they did say that they would be contacting an Embassy and to leave photocopies of the messages. We don't know what the outcome was.

Jill eventually found me in later that evening and explained what had happened. She handed me the original handwriting, and though I didn't understand it I was very intrigued. A few days later a very excited Jill visited me and said that she had received a translation from the very source that had originated it.

We subsequently became very good friends with the family and we have helped each other in many ways. Regarding the automatic writing that Jill had done, I passed it on to Dr. Hanny (co-author of the book, 'The Search for Omseti') who is a leading authority in Cairo. He had great access to scholars who could translate every known form of writing. The reply that I received back from Dr. Hanny was that he had only seen similar writing once in his entire life. It was on the 'Gates of the Sun' in Peru.

While I was on my first visit to Jill's family, my wife had received a call at home from the television studio. A man had telephoned them leaving his number, asking me to contact him urgently. I rang this man, he told me that he was twenty seven years old and was suffering from ME. He said that as far as he was concerned his life was finished because he was so ill, all of his muscles were weak and consequently he felt absolutely useless. What concerned him most was the numerous prescribed drugs that had poisoned his blood. Clearly, his severe allergies and their treatments had left his whole immune system sadly depleted. He asked if I could help him. Initially he was apprehensive of calling as he wasn't sure of what he might be getting into. He said that he didn't want to be taken away by aliens!

His mother had watched the show with him and could relate to a lot of the things I had said, it was she who reassured her son to speak to me. I explained to him, as I do to everyone, that I am not a healer, as some people claim. I am not exactly sure what happens. I just know that if I ask for help it usually comes. However I do get a sign from my Orion friends as to whether or not people or animals will be all right when I have asked for help. I did feel sorry for this young man. I said that I'd had a very busy day so far and that I would like a few days to absorb what he had been telling me. I told him that I would ring him back at the end of the week.

Well, it seemed that he couldn't wait till then because he rang me back. Apparently, after about an hour of our first conversation, he became very excited. Whilst talking to me he felt very mellowed and a smell of gunpowder came off his body. He felt really good, the best he had felt for a long time. He asked lots of questions, though pleasantly confused, he was very happy.

Other people have also spoken to me about the smell this young man had described. It has been described as a sulphurous sort of smell. I believe that this occurs because all the toxins leave the person's body, just as the toxins from this particular man's blood, left his body. I wasn't sure if he was cured, but I certainly knew something was happening. I was very pleased and kept in contact with him. The latest update is that he feels that he does not require hospital treatment. He wasn't sure what he should tell the doctors, but remarked that they couldn't understand the sudden transformation. He had decided to simply tell them that he had visited a 'faith healer'. He felt that this would be acceptable. This man did say something to me that I did find interesting. Apparently at certain times of the day he felt a presence with him, and he could ask it to come and go whenever he wanted. He was not frightened by it.

I have subsequently done other TV and radio broadcasts. The sceptics are so annoying because they have such closed minds. I will not get involved with them anymore. I only do shows and lectures with scientists, astronomers etc. The subject is too important to be ridiculed or debunked.

VERIFICATION

'My name is Don from Birmingham. Here is an account of my experiences with Terry Walters.

'In early April of 1994 I was in my bedroom one morning, when I put the portable TV on to find that 'The Time the Place' programme was on 0, and the subject under discussion was UFOs and extra-terrestrials. Having recently acquired an interest in the subject I went downstairs and began to videotape the programme. I watched the programme to the end and took the tape out of the machine and moved on to my usual business of coping with a

distressing illness.

'Since 1987 I have been living with severe food allergies, a chronic systemic yeast infection called Candidiasis and also at times
chronic viral infections lasting several months. I played 'The
Time, The Place' programme several times over the next two or
three days, and slowly it dawned on me that there was a man on
the programme talking about extra-terrestrials's curing people of
serious illnesses. I decided that if aliens were prepared to help
people with their health problems, it was the kind of help I
would like to have so I phoned Yorkshire Television who gave me
Anglia Television's number. I phoned 'ATV' and they passed my
phone number and name on to Terry Walters. As I was talking to
Terry over the phone I started to feel very sedated, tranquil and
relaxed. I also noted an incredible strong smell in the room that
smelt like sulphur or gunpowder - it was as if someone had been
firing a rifle in the kitchen it was so strong.

'I felt so sedated I had to go upstairs and lay down on my bed
with my eyes closed. I knew something very profound had happened and I felt quite concerned that I'd got myself in big trouble!

'Several months later, I was talking over the phone again with
Terry, and in bed that night I noticed that whenever I put the
night lamp on to look at the clock near my bed, there was an
orange colour in front of my eyes for a few seconds. I knew I'd
been given a second 'treatment' which for obvious reasons I
called 'orange'. For the past two years now Terry's friends have
been helping me - it's been very tough as my problems have
become very severe but I am able to keep going because I feel
with the help of Terry's friends I could still get better.'

Don

CHAPTER 6

My Orion Friends, their Craft and Space Travel

I feel that we are being visited by extra-terrestrials from more than one planet. The male Orions that I communicate with are taller than normal human beings, at least six feet tall. Their skin is tanned and leathery looking. They have five fingers which are long and slender. Their hair is thick and blonde, and is usually worn shoulder length. Their overall facial appearance is quite similar to ours, with the exception of their higher cheekbones and stunning, almost hypnotic large blue eyes. The females are equally beautiful, slim, but very strong. On the bottom of their feet they have lots of little suckers, similar to those on an octopus's tentacle, but much smaller.

I normally communicate with the Orions telepathically, but on the rare occasions they speak to me, it is in English. However I get the impression that they can communicate in any language. The Orions internal organs are higher up in their bodies than humans, and are more compact. They live to an old age. Due to their diet, they appear to have eradicated germs and disease from their planet, which is within the Orion Constellation.

I must make it clear I can only describe what I see, from the way the Orions present themselves to me. They could of course be tricking me into believing they look like this, so that they may be considered more presentable. The particular group of extra-terrestrials I communicate with, are, according to Ufologists, known as the 'Nordics', because of their Norwegian appearance. Some people have referred to them as 'Angels'. This is the title I prefer, because of the remarkable things they do and because I know they are here for the good of mankind.

One of the many things they have led me to do is warn

people of possible danger, put me in touch with spirits and help people with illness - some are terminal. The illnesses they have cured are almost beyond belief. More details of these incidents will be explained in later chapters. My angelic friends take me up to certain points in the past and future, and show me what's happening around the world. The chapter in this book entitled 'The Asia Trip' is one such journey.

The events and situations I am made privy to, are usually of extreme importance, and are often areas of the world that my 'friends' are very worried about; especially countries that are going to experience a forthcoming earthquake or volcanic eruption etc. When I witness these impending disasters I draw pictures of them, they may be of countries, towns, bridges or water disasters. What occurs is exactly the image or message I was presented with. My pictures are also a way for me to come to terms with the fact that these things are really happening.

After certain disasters I get the distinct impression that my friends do help, I've seen them through my mind repairing damage done to the earth. I am shown so many things on a daily basis that it seems an impossible task to write about it all. A lot of the information I am given I cannot do anything about, as I believe this would get me into trouble. I can and do warn friends, family and acquaintances. After telling them, they are able to take precautions.

The Orions are very spiritual beings. I believe that in a way they are 'the past, the present and the future'. They have a vast knowledge of this Earth and other similar planets. Earth is part of a system and if we destroy it, it will cause a serious 'knock on' effect to the rest of the system's planets. This is one of the reasons why they want to save the Earth. My understanding of the Orions is that they are capable of doing **anything**; for example; from altering people's minds and their way of thinking, to altering and maintaining the universe. They are like our 'Caretakers'.

I have never had an experience with the grey small aliens I have heard so much about from other people. I feel sorry for those individuals who have had bad contacts with them. I know how hard it must be to explain to other people, that you have no control over being abducted by extra-terrestrials, who do intimate, unpleasant things to you. To many abductees this must bring a big change in their lives and in many instances trauma. My experience with my Orion friends is not one of abduction, I go voluntarily.

Wherever I may be in this country, or in any part of the world, I know if the Orions are present. Through telepathy I feel their presence, like whales who can communicate over vast distances in the sea. I feel that my 'friends' contact me from a planet inside the Orion constellation in much the same way.

It is my belief that some Orions are living on Earth as family units. I've heard reports of these beings living in America, they have had medical tests conducted and it was found, as I said previously, that their internal organs are higher set and more compact inside their bodies than humans. They were also found to have an extra rib. These extra-terrestrials communicate to each other through telepathy and are able to speak.

I'd now like to say something about the spacecraft. The general appearance and structure of the spacecraft I see get updated, like our motor cars. I have seen the changes. The early craft were a silvery grey colour on the outside with fewer portholes than the present ones. These portholes were also more square. The transparent material was very thick and difficult to see out of. I can speak from experience as I have been on board these spacecraft. The outer covering was thin but strong and the craft had small rooms. The walls were made in some sort of honeycomb design. The best way I can describe the finished surface, was that it was covered in a leaf like pattern, with blue and yellow colouring. The size of the craft was about forty feet across by fifteen feet tall, there were two floors accommodating three to five crew members.

The updated craft has three floors, it is about twenty five feet tall with a fifty five feet diameter and has a slightly domed-shaped top. The inside is much the same as the earlier version but slightly bigger with not so many compartments. It has many more port holes than previous craft.

As the bright white light shines out of the portholes it forms the appearance of a white halo around the ship. The colour of the craft is a striking blue-green. It looks like brushed aluminium. The ships have what looks like a mass of navigation lights outside. These lights actually pulse in accordance with the workings of the reactor inside the ship. The craft now appear to have hydraulic tripod landing legs. The compliment of these ships vary from five to seven crew.

The Orion craft is powered by a reactor in the centre of it, which is mounted on the second 'floor'. A device coming out of it goes down through to the ground floor, where there are three amplifiers which rotate to direct the ship. It works both on an anti-gravity and anti-matter system and is powered I believe by a powdered crystal, which is the main element to fuel the reactor.

The craft travels in time when they enter the Earth's atmosphere and turn over and fly at a 45° angle. They have their own magnetic field. Prior to entering the Earth's atmosphere, the Orion ships travel through corridors in space, that are like a type of warp. I have calculated that the ships can travel from a planet within the cluster of Orion to Earth in less than eight days. It could even be eight hours! Scientists are investigating warped space travel at present. The speed of light is altogether different in space, more than we could ever imagine. Maybe it's the speed of dark!

By regulating the speed of their craft and using reverse gravity, an Orion ship can drop like a stone onto this planet,

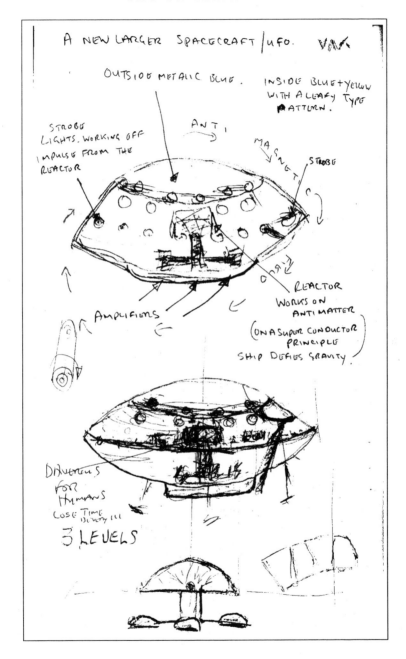

A NEW LARGER SPACECRAFT / UFO. VM

OUTSIDE METALIC BLUE.

INSIDE BLUE + YELLOW
WITH A LEAFY TYPE
PATTERN.

STROBE
LIGHTS. WORKING OFF
IMPULSE FROM THE
REACTOR

ANT

MAGNET

STROBE

REACTOR
WORKS ON
ANTI MATTER
(ON A SUPER CONDUCTOR
PRINCIPLE
SHIP DEFIES GRAVITY.

AMPLIFIERS

DANGEROUS
FOR
HUMANS
LOSE TIME
3 LEVELS

64

but they can control the speed of descent. By reversing the gravity they can take off from Earth incredibly fast. I should mention at this point that Orions use odd numbers in their mathematical formulas to create energy. Though they have managed to harness this energy aboard their craft, if it got out of control the effects would be catastrophic, similar to that of a nuclear bomb explosion.

Whilst travelling, the UFOs can appear to look like 'glowing jelly'. They appear to distort and change into different shapes. What I am reporting is not anything I've read or watched on television, or video, or gleaned from anyone else's information, it is what I see and know. You don't have to be a special person to see a UFO. Most people have probably witnessed them go through the sky, but have not recognised them. If they saw one close at hand they would be left in no doubt.

UFOs have been around for thousands, if not millions of years, it is not simply a current trend or something for the sceptical to ridicule. This phenomenon should be looked at seriously. It is part of our lives and future. **They are here** whether we accept it or not.

CHAPTER 7

Asia Trip

During the early hours of one October morning in 1992 I was awoken by my Orion friends. In my mind I knew that they were around and up to something. Then I felt compelled to look out of my bedroom window and look at the sky. On doing so I observed several UFOS. In my mind I asked them what they were doing and where they were travelling to. They replied that I would not know the geographical location.

By now the beings from the UFOS were communicating with me very vividly. However my wife Dianne was getting concerned and asked what was happening, so I related to her the telepathic conversation the Orions and I were having. I asked them if it would be possible for Dianne to see their craft, they said 'Yes' and they told me to tell Dianne to look at the 'Seven Sisters' star cluster because their craft would be seen quite clearly. They also said that they were slowing down to five thousand miles per hour and coming in above Herefordshire. At this point both Dianne and I gazed intently in the direction we had been told. Dianne said to me, 'But Terry I can't see them'. When I asked my 'friends' for further help, they told me to tell Dianne to look deeper and closer into the 'Seven Sisters' constellation*; and sure enough we both saw at least five craft moving fast across the sky.

The UFOS could be described as looking like white tadpoles. Though they were some distance away I am convinced that they were definitely the Orions flying craft. I then asked if I could travel with them, and they said I could. Here is my experience of travelling with them tele-

* The Pleiades

pathically, whilst standing at my bedroom window with my wife:

The journey I embarked upon was extremely intense. Although the ship had a crew, I communicated with only one of them, a male, who I could see. As I was travelling with my 'friends' I explained to Dianne step by step what I could see and what I was experiencing. They told me that after leaving Herefordshire they would be journeying five thousand miles eastbound to Asia, to a point near the 63rd parallel. We were now travelling across Asia. I could clearly see the Ural mountain range, and as we passed them, forests and other sights; I narrated this all to my wife. As the craft appeared to be coming to a halt the Orion asked 'What's that running around on the Earth?' He had noticed something he had not seen before. I said that they were horses. Earlier I had told Dianne that this place was very cold, and she now begged the question 'Could these animals be reindeer?' but I could see that they were definitely horses.

This incredible journey lasted only a few minutes before we reached our destination. The craft landed and two Orions got out. There was a lot of snow and the Orion who had asked about the horses shielded his eyes, as if he found the light too bright. I got the distinct impression that this Orion had not been to our planet before. The other Orion put what looked like a big tube into the ground. He seemed to be taking a soil sample. We returned and I remember reboarding the craft. We took off and hovered about tree top level.

The craft now shone a beam of light down onto the ground. I was very curious and asked the Orions if people could see this, they said that both the light and the craft would be visible. I had never seen a UFO shine a beam of light down before. I was absolutely astonished. At this point my Orion friend told me that at the time their mothership was in the vicinity. They said that out of their mothership three hundred smaller craft came to visit our world and that

This is what I drew of the 'tool' the Alien put in the ground to extract Earth.

they would be around for six weeks.

One alarming fact that my Orion friend told me, was that three Orions were being held near Bedford, in an R.A.F. base. They asked me when I was going to visit them?

In what seemed only a matter of minutes my mind returned to normal and once again I was in the silence and calm of my bedroom, with Dianne standing next to me. Getting back into bed, we both felt extremely confused and tired. We awoke early in the morning, full of emotion about what had happened, as the experience had been very profound. Without doubt, what had happened a few hours previously was real.

We decided to try and make sense of it all by examining a World Atlas, and by piecing something together some of the facts. The atlas we had was a good one and we gleaned quite a lot of information from it. First of all we measured five thousand miles, starting from Herefordshire and going across Asia - which was east. We counted up the latitude lines to the area where the Orions and I had visited. It was

Siberia. At first I could not be certain that we were measuring correctly, but then I knew nothing about the parallel lines of latitude. However I had the feeling that when my Orion friends show or tell me something they always 'put it across correctly'. As I looked at the contours and features of the atlas, I knew undoubtedly this was the 'place' I had visited.

The place in Siberia was called Yakutsk, and I wondered why I should be made aware of this tiny place. The atlas revealed other things about this place. It said Yakutsk was noted for its horse breeding, its extreme cold and its mineral content. Still very baffled, my wife and I took our dog for a walk and spoke at length, each trying to piece together the whole episode.

After our walk we went to visit a friend whose name is Doreen. Immediately upon entering Doreen's lounge I knew that she was going to be of help. This is a classic way that the Orions work with me. If they do not show me certain things in their entirety they will make me visit places where I would not ordinarily go. Somebody will always be around in these places to help me put the puzzle together. This was indeed what my 'friends' were doing at this time.

Doreen had absolutely piles of books in her home stacked everywhere. I was thinking; with all of that literature about, she must be quite knowledgeable. So I asked if she knew about the 63rd parallel in the Yakutsk region. Doreen said that it was a famous weak spot on the Earth, a fault line, where the tectonic plates rub together. She said that it is one of the most delicate places on the planet. Doreen asked me if I had bought that Sunday's, 'Mail on Sunday' newspaper. I replied that I had not. She said that she didn't think that she had thrown her copy out, so we searched through a pile of paperwork on the floor and with luck we found it. She said, 'Turn to the centre pages'. To my astonishment it reported all about a little place called Yakutsk.

As I was reading the article it said that this place was so

remote that it had only recently been mapped. This is probably why the Orions said that I wouldn't know where it was, when I had asked them where they were going. The article went on to confirm many of the things that I had said: the temperature drops to -70°C in the winter time, and that it was an extremely difficult place to get to in mid-winter. Yet in this 'hell' of a place the Yakutsk Russian Mafia thrived.

My mind was working overtime as to what was going to unfold. I could not wait to read on. The newspaper reported that huge amounts of diamonds were being mined in Yakutsk. As the ground was so cold, huge explosives were being used to penetrate the frozen ground. The story went on to say that the place was being blown up 'like there was no tomorrow'. The diamonds were being sold so cheaply because of the quantity being mined that 'De Beers' the diamond merchant was worried that the whole diamond industry was being turned upside down. The Russian Mafia was, and still is mining the diamonds, and to quote the newspaper 'selling them like sweets from Woolworth'.

I was now beginning to see why the Orions had taken me to this place. They could see the danger of what was happening in Siberia. The Earth's crust can only stand so much. The Orions were worried that the huge explosions could trigger off this weak area, an explosion so great, it could wipe Asia off the map and even tilt the world off its axis.

Parts of the puzzle were now beginning to unravel. I thanked Doreen and went home with much on my mind to sort out. By now it was lunch time. I put the television on and low and behold a trailer advertising a Channel 4 television programme that evening, called 'Dispatches' came on. The programme was going to reveal the truth behind the diamond mining in Russia.

As you can see, a pattern was emerging, solving the mystery of why the Orions had visited that night, but I still didn't know what the beam of light being shone down from the Orion craft was for.

Later that afternoon I had to visit our local Conservative Office to pick up some paperwork, as I was chairman of the branch. When I entered the office I was once again 'taken aback', there staring straight at me, on a large desk, was a big book about 'De Beers' and diamonds. Apparently our local MP had just recently had a meeting with 'De Beers' and had left the book in the office. To me all of these clues were part of the jigsaw. The Orions are trying to warn me about the vulnerability of this part of the world.

Early that evening my wife and I decided to go shopping in a local large warehouse. This store contains almost everything. I went straight to the book department to find, right under my nose, a thick book all about UFOs. I flicked over the pages and there it was, a flying saucer over the sky of Japan shining down a beam of light over an earthquake damaged area. The beam of light was repairing it! I then realised that this is what they were doing in Yakutsk. It is as I have tried to explain, the Orions that I see are looking after us and our planet. The UFO book went on to say the UFOs are sighted frequently, shining these beams of light down over disaster areas. Let's hope Siberia remains safe. I think it's pretty precarious there. Is there something in the phrase, 'forewarned is forearmed'. I have since discovered that Doreen worked for 'De Beers' a few years ago in Germany. Which seems quite a coincidence.

A few days later, I heard banging during the night. I thought someone was knocking on my front door. However I telepathically observed three Orions, two men and one woman, banging on the walls of a room. They were very frightened and asking me to get them out. I noticed that they were wearing dark blue jumpers which were not their own clothes.

Stewart, my son-in-law, came to my house the next evening. He was completely unaware of my recent telepathic journey, which made what he had to say the more interesting. As a courier, Stewart had often driven past an R.A.F. base in Bedfordshire, known as the 'home of the Harrier'. Like all military installations it was well guarded but Stewart said he used to be able to drive very close to the base without any problem. What had surprised Stewart, and why he was telling me this story, was that the base had suddenly become heavily guarded, with razor wire fencing being erected. Now he could get nowhere near the place.

I was surprised but not at all shocked by this revelation. Stewart had obviously come to my house that night with some kind of message, perhaps from my 'friends'. Was this the place where the captured Orions were being held? I must reiterate that the only reason my son-in-law visited me that evening was to tell me of the astonishing changes at the base. Unfortunately, although this news helped to confirm the plight of the Orions, there was nothing that I could do.

Mandy

During 1986, I started to keep more of a diary of the paranormal events that were taking place in my life. Many people had asked me to help them with their inexplicable experiences and illnesses. I knew I wasn't mad; credible people were placing their trust in me, and this helped me to deal with my life.

Mandy was a school friend of my youngest daughter Angela. They had been close friends since they both started senior school. The girls were sixteen years old, just getting ready to leave school for college. One evening Angela telephoned Mandy's house to arrange to go out. Angela was shocked when the telephone was answered by a very distressed au-pair, who was employed by Mandy's parents. She said that Mandy had been rushed to the local hospital with meningitis. We were all terribly upset. Angela was advised to ring again in the morning for any news.

We went to bed feeling very sad. That night I was awakened from my sleep with the worst headache I've ever had. I said to Dianne, 'I feel like my brain is exploding'. It took me ages to go back to sleep, all sorts of things were going through my mind. In the morning when I felt it was late enough and the right time to ring, I asked Angela to telephone Mandy's house and get an update on the situation. The au-pair once again picked up the telephone and said that Mandy had taken a turn for the worse, her brain had enlarged and was bleeding, and she had been transferred to the Atkinson Morley hospital in South West London. Apparently Mandy had the worst form of meningitis, she was very seriously ill. I now knew that the horrendous pain that I had experienced, was in fact me taking on Mandy's illness. I definitely felt that I needed to help Mandy. I wasn't quite sure what I was meant to do, but I knew I would be guided. So I just took things as they came. I did feel that this was a very big problem, and I asked myself the question - did I need extra help?

At this point I want to mention something that occurred two weeks prior to this incident. I was at a function in my capacity as a Town Councillor, when a lady approached me. She asked me who I was. At first I was teasing and I didn't tell her. The lady tried several times to get me to introduce myself, when finally a friend came up and put her out of her misery. She said, 'Vicky meet Terry', and consequently we spoke for a little while. Vicky said she was pleased we had met and said, 'Hope to see you soon'.

I was still thinking a great deal about Mandy and what had happened to me. I had a very bad day, worrying about what I could do. That night, just before dawn I felt myself leaving my body. This was the first time that I could vividly remember this happening. I woke Dianne as I sat up. I could see Mandy laying in her bed, I was looking down on her, she was in what looked like a sort of portakabin. I drew what I saw. I could see Mandy having difficulty with the respirator tube in her throat, so I told her through my mind to pull it out, this she did and she started to breathe. I was quite over-whelmed. I remember feeling quite exhausted by the experience. I felt I needed to ring the hospital, I had to find out what had happened, I knew this experience was for real - I wasn't dreaming! I telephoned the hospital, and said to the staff that I was a close family friend, and I was immediately put through to Sister Francis. I had actually met Sister Francis before. Sister Francis had looked after Mandy's little sister, when she was very ill. She had taken care of her while she stayed at a nursing home to give her parents respite care. Unfortunately, Mandy's sister had died and it was at the funeral that I met Sister Francis. I said to Sister Francis that we had met, and she said 'What do you want to tell me'. I proceeded to reiterate what had happened to me regarding

Mandy and the tracheotomy respirator tube. Sister Francis then asked me when this had happened. I told her and she said, 'Yes, Mandy did pull the tube at the time you said. She is now making progress, but is still very ill, please carry on praying for her'. I said I certainly would. Sister Francis then told me that the parents were taking a walk in the hospital grounds, otherwise I could have spoken to them.

Something was looking after Mandy, I knew it, it was my Orion friends working through me; there was a lot to be sorted out and I felt it would be very wearing. Meanwhile Dianne and I had made an appointment to look at a house we were interested in buying; but before we left I decided to telephone Dianne's relative Charlie (see Chapter Two) to explain what had happened to me during the night. I managed to get through to him, which was a bit of good luck as he is usually not available during working hours. This particular day he had taken off work as he was not feeling very well. As I explained to him what had happened, he responded; 'Terry, I know these things happen to you, but it was very dangerous of you to leave your body like that, this whole thing is too much for you on your own, you need help'. Before signing off he wished Mandy and me well.

As a result of this telephone call we were late in arriving at the house for the viewing. I rang the door bell and a lady answered it. I was quite surprised to find that the lady was Vicky, the person who had been intent on being introduced to me. As Dianne was looking at her watch Vicky said, 'Don't worry about being late', and invited us in. Dianne briefly explained why we were late, and Vicky replied, You haven't come to buy my house, you need help'. I thought to myself, this is what I had just been told on the phone ten minutes earlier, perhaps she was the help.

Vicky asked us to join her around a table and join hands. This event included a rather bewildered estate agent. Apparently Vicky comes from a religious family, her father was a vicar. As we all held hands she said something like this: 'Let's pray for Mandy to get well, may the blood turn to water and run out of her head'. Although I am not particularly religious, I was grateful to Vicky. It's the power that's important, maybe it is all the same power from one source - though most people cannot accept this idea yet. I can still see this meeting in my mind, the estate agent was very close to tears. No one was upset about our disinterest in the house, and we became very good friends with Vicky and still keep in contact.

Feeling somewhat easier in my body and mind I went about my daily business, but when I went to bed I was still quite bothered. It must have been around the same time, about 4 a.m. when I saw Mandy again. As before I sat up and told Dianne; 'Mandy's eyes have briefly opened and she's moved her right arm'. I was both very excited and confused; I couldn't wait to ring the hospital. The same procedure happened; Sister Francis spoke to me, she said that Mandy's parents were not there at that moment, they had gone to get some breakfast, and went on to say that they were in good spirits. I stopped her, and told her what I had seen, she replied, 'Exactly, that did happen and at the time you said'. Both of us exchanged thanks and I said that I would contact the parents in a few day's time.

I did not feel the urge to enquire about Mandy for a little while, I thought I would wait until I felt it necessary to ring again. The next news I heard came from Angela, she said that Mandy was home. Her parents said that it was a miracle, since she was the only person at that time to have come out of the Intensive Care ward alive! I telephoned the family and asked if I could visit Mandy. We made arrangements for the next day. When I saw her, she was a little emotional, Mandy came up to me and said that she had seen me come to her in hospital, she had heard my voice. Her father handed me some photographs that he had taken of her whilst she was all wired up on the machine in the Intensive

Care ward. I'm glad he did, because when I saw them I recognised the room, it was the place I had visited when I was 'out of my body'. Dianne also looked at the photographs and agreed that they were just like the pictures I had drawn. Everyone was elated with Mandy's progress. I felt overwhelmingly that there was still more I could do. I thought I ought to buy her a cross and chain, believing this might help. This story continues in to the next chapter.

CHAPTER 9

The Cottage

A few months after Mandy got well in mid June, I received a telephone call from Wales, it was Doreen, my mother-in-law. She said that she was ringing from a farm in Abergavenny, where she and her husband had parked their caravan. Although my mother-in-law was enjoying the rest and countryside she thought it would be good to have some company. She suggested that if Dianne and I left early enough, we could come up to Wales, 'make a nice day of it' and spend some time with them. I quite liked the sound of that and started to make arrangements. I asked some friends, John and Isabel if they would like to join us, since a few days earlier they had been talking about visiting John's relatives in Wales. I thought that we could combine the two trips.

I recalled that Mandy's father had a holiday cottage in a village in Wales. I decided to give him a call to see if we could rent the cottage for a couple of days, as its location was perfect. The cottage was situated between Abergavenny and John's relation's place. I contacted Mandy's father who said that we would be welcome to have the cottage. However, he warned me that builders were removing a chimney stack, and there was a general mess about the cottage as he was doing it up. The key was with his neighbour, so he would contact him to let him know that we were coming. However, Mandy's father said that if we arrived after 9 p.m. we shouldn't need to disturb his neighbour, a quiet man who liked to go to bed early, because the key to the cottage would be left in the door.

All was going to plan. I confirmed with Doreen, that we were on our way to Abergavenny. We arrived and spent some time with the family, but before the evening closed we decided we ought to head for the cottage. Before we left, we arranged for the in-laws to visit us at the cottage the following day. We agreed to meet at noon and I gave them a plan of how to find us.

It was well past 9 p.m. before we arrived at the cottage. We drew up outside but could not find a parking place, so we parked the car some distance away. We had to carry our cases up a little path which passed by another cottage, and as we did so, we noticed people peeping at us from behind their curtains. We didn't disturb the immediate neighbour who looked after the key, and as agreed the key was left in the lock of the door.

We had a quick look at the place and could see that some repairs and alterations were taking place. Mandy's bedroom however was in good order. There were several bibles around the rooms and I remember thinking that perhaps Mandy's family might be Roman Catholics. Mandy's bedroom was so warm and inviting but only had a single bed in it, so we could not use that room. Mandy's parent's bedroom was not being worked on, so I suggested that it would be a good room for John and Isabel to have. Dianne and I took the other double bedroom but it was rather upside down, with wallpaper half stripped off and pots of paint strewn everywhere. There were two single beds, so I pushed them together; it would suit us fine as we were only expecting to stay for a couple of days.

Dianne and Isabel decided to play a board game, there were several on the shelves in the dining room. They selected a game at random, one that comprised of a cube containing letters and a sand timer. The object of the game was to shake the cube allowing a random slection of letters to turn face up and from these letters the players each made up as many words as possible before the sand ran out of time. Along with the game there was some paper which had already been used, some words and letters were in red ink others in blue and, as Dianne and Isabel could not find any clean paper, they used this to play on.

The game only lasted for about fifteen minutes. Dianne and Isabel were not very happy with the words they could make from the letters that kept turning face up. They were horrible words like 'Devil', 'Evil' and 'Satan'. Subsequently they both decided to call it a day and went to bed ahead of John and I. Since word games were not something John or I particularly enjoy, we had switched the television on and watched it for a short while before joining our wives in bed.

As expected, the next morning we were woken by the builders. I pulled back the curtains, it was a beautiful day and I admired the lovely view, lots of rolling countryside, it was very pleasant. Whilst looking out of the window, one workman called over - 'Good morning', I returned his greeting and he asked if we had slept okay, I replied, 'Yes thanks'.

I heard John and Isabel getting up, so Dianne and I got dressed and met them down stairs. We decided to buy some milk and something to cook for breakfast from the local store. We went outside and walked down the path. Dianne tried to take a photograph of the cottage but the camera would not work properly; this seemed a little odd, as there had been no previous trouble with it. Isabel said, 'Don't worry, I'll take some photos and you can have the negatives'. She also attempted to take a picture but her camera refused to work too. John checked it, thinking that maybe he had not loaded it properly, but he couldn't find anything wrong with it. It all seemed rather strange.

We carried on walking to the store and passed the neighbour. We introduced ourselves and thanked him for leaving the key. He asked us if we'd slept alright and we told him that we had. The next person we passed was a lady who had been peeping from her curtains the previous evening, realising that we were guests of Mandy's parents, she smiled and acknowledged us. Then she asked us if we'd slept alright.

We arrived at the local store. It was a friendly place, so we

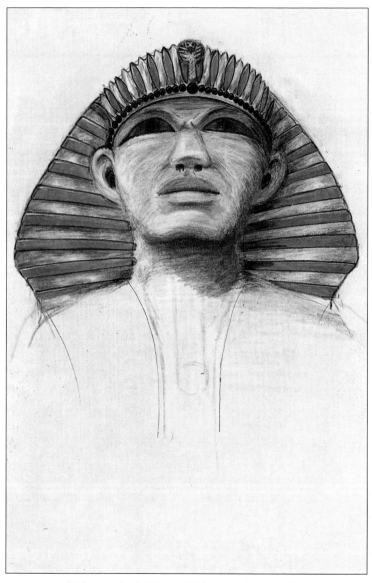

*This is the Sphinx which is how it would
have been thousands of years ago, as it was portrayed
through my Orion friends*

1

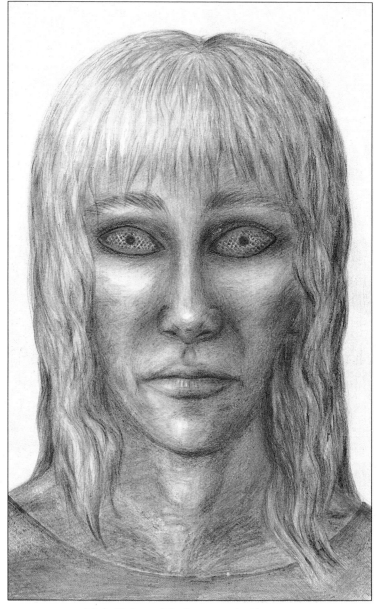

Male Orion with the very piercing eyes

Female Orion with hypnotic eyes

Above Terry and Dianne with Robert Bauval, November 1995

Left Excavation in front of Sphinx with Robert by water cover. November 1995

4

View of Giza Plateaux

Cheops, November 1995

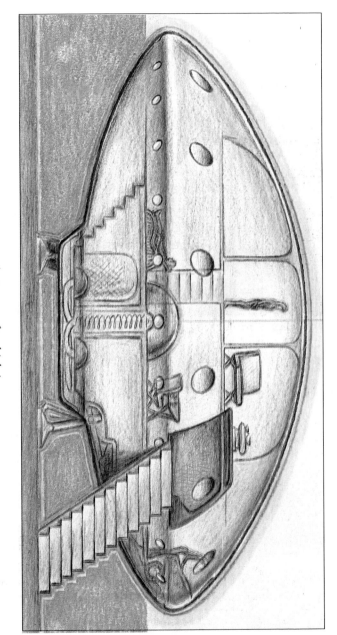

A spacecraft which is typical of the kind used by aliens to visit our planet

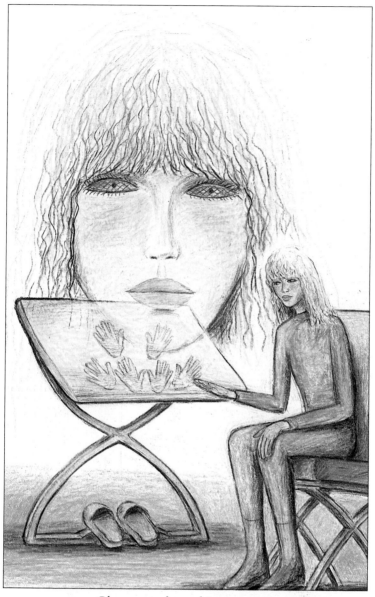

Glass control panel in spacecraft
manufactured from gold.

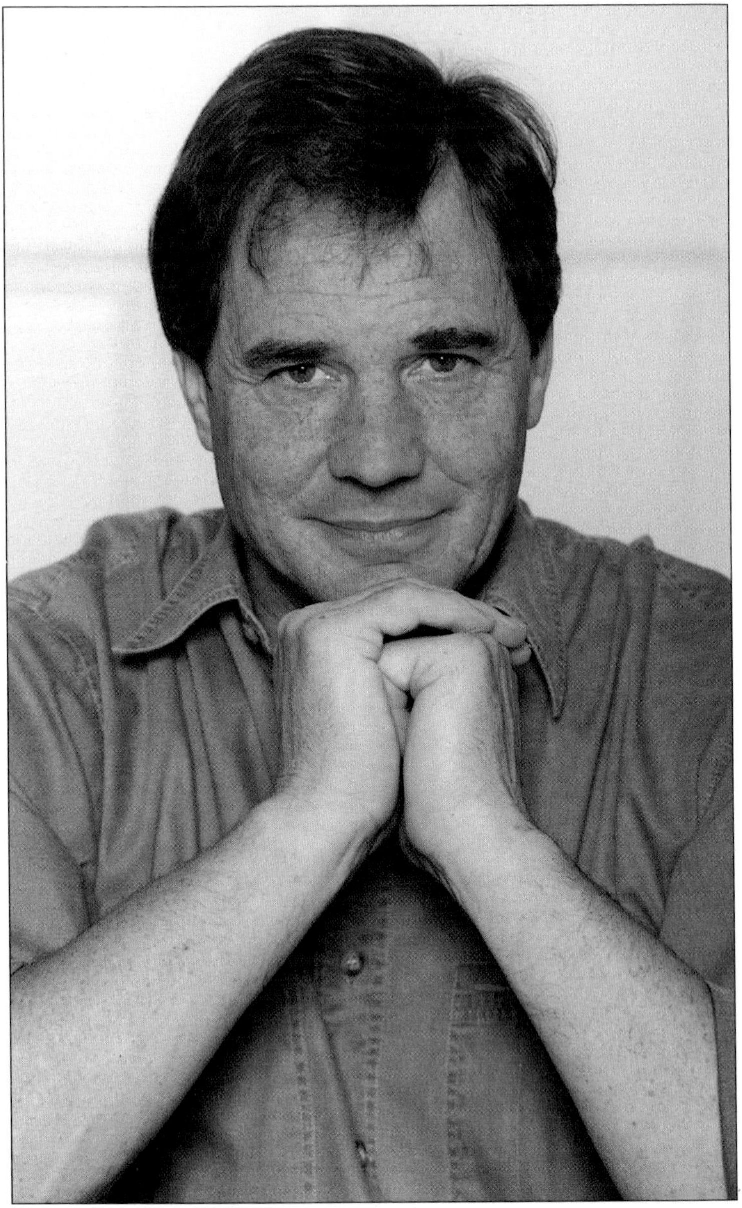

Terry Walters

introduced ourselves and told the shop keeper where we were staying. As he was serving us he asked the same question: 'How did you sleep?' I remember wondering, 'Why is everyone so interested in whether we slept well or not'? We decided as it was such a lovely morning we would take a stroll, rather than going straight back to the cottage for breakfast.

There was a pretty lane nearby with a pottery so we decided to visit it. The views across the hills were superb. Both Isabel and Dianne decided to try and take some photos and to their amazement and delight their cameras functioned perfectly. It appeared that just the cottage objected to its picture being taken!

We returned to the cottage and cooked breakfast then lounged about in the garden. We found some sunbeds, and relaxed. It was not long before my in-laws arrived so I got up and showed them around. John my father-in-law was happy to sit in the sun, but Doreen was interested in looking around, as I was by now. We walked around to the back of the cottage. We both looked up to one of the rear windows. I saw something spooky there, it was an elderly man wearing a straw hat, I turned to Doreen who gave me a knowing glance. It was obvious that she had seen something too.

Later that afternoon, John and Doreen got ready to return to Abergavenny. Dianne and Doreen tidied up, but as they were about to take the sunbeds back through the cottage door, Doreen said; 'Get behind me Satan!' To Dianne it was a horrible and sinister thing to say and seemed totally out of context. But it clearly showed that Doreen had seen and felt something she did not like that afternoon.

Dianne's parents had long gone by now and the evening was closing in. I thought it would be nice to have a meal with Dianne and our friends down at the local pub. After enjoying a good meal we decided to take a walk before

returning to the cottage. There were several lanes and turn-
ings which we could have explored but my intuition led me
to take an unattractive route because I knew I needed to go
there. As we proceeded we came across a sign on the grass,
it was the name-sign of the village where we were staying. I
asked Dianne and Isabel if they could create any words from
it, which was strange, considering I don't usually like playing word games. Anyway Dianne and Isabel couldn't create
any interesting words, so they abandoned the game.

After getting back to the cottage Isabel said that she
wanted to telephone her daughter to make sure that she was
all right, but she was unable to get a decent line out. The
telephone was playing up so she left it and decided to try
again in the morning. John and I thought we would watch a
boxing match on the television but Dianne and Isabel were
not interested, so they went to bed and left us to it. We tried
to tune into the TV station but the picture was extremely
poor and became worse. It was impossible to watch, so we
decided to join our partners in bed.

As I was walking up the stairs the air at one particular spot
turned very cold. I went back down and looked under it and
saw a concrete section beneath; paying no more attention I
continued on to my bedroom. Despite the fact that it was
June 21st; a warm summer's solstice evening, I felt cold.

As I entered the bedroom Dianne said that she had pulled
out a magazine from a pile on the landing, and had found
two interesting articles. The first article was about garlic and
the second about why people build round houses: to keep
the devil out of the corners. After hearing this and reflecting
on the other events of the evening, I had the distinct feeling
that something was not as it should be. In the meantime
Dianne had taken a piece of paper and a pencil to bed with
her in case she found a word game to do inside the magazine. I got into bed and fell asleep but only for a short while.

It must have been just after midnight when l awoke and
saw a shimmering figure by my bed. It was quite stocky and

bear like, it came forward and then backed off and disappeared when I stared at it. I felt I needed the protection of my Orion friends at this point. I should add, that at this time in my life no one knew about my 'friends'.

Suddenly the creature appeared and leapt over me straight onto Dianne. It seemed to be trying to suffocate her, so I quickly instructed Dianne through my mind to scream very loudly. I believe that my friends from Orion were also telling her to do the same thing. We knew that a high pitch noise would frighten the creature away. I did not physically shake Dianne to wake her, I knew the scream would have the same effect.

Dianne screamed louder than anyone I have ever heard. She awoke terrified, not knowing what was happening or even why she had screamed. I explained why. Then Dianne said she could taste blood in her throat and she thought that probably, the intense scream had caused it. Panic then set in because Dianne could not feel her legs - they were numb, and she said that the expression on my face was frightening her. I explained to Dianne that even though I had wanted her to scream, when she did, it was so loud that it frightened the life out of me. I proceeded tactfully to say I had seen something. I did not mention what the creature looked like or that it had been trying to get to her, only that it was present and I was warding it off.

We felt that we should visit John and Isabel to ensure that everything was okay, particularly as Dianne had screamed so loudly. I wondered if they might be even too frightened to come out of their bedroom. Dianne could not walk because her legs were still numb, so I rubbed them and tried to get the blood circulating properly. Then I steadied Dianne across the landing towards John and Isabel's bedroom and knocked on their door. There was no reply. I made several attempts to arouse them but to no avail. I decided to open the door and to our astonishment they were both in a deep sleep. Dianne and I found this incomprehensible since the scream under normal circumstances would have woken anyone.

I had to shake Isabel for quite a while but eventually she stirred. I explained that Dianne had woken up screaming because of a bad dream and we had decided to check up on them in case they thought she had been injured or even murdered. However, Isabel said she had heard nothing and suggested we go downstairs to make some tea. Sensing that things were far from all right I suggested that Isabel went back to sleep, besides, she looked very drowsy.

Dianne needed to visit the toilet and I offered to go with her but she said no. However, I knew I had to protect Dianne. As she crossed the landing to find the toilet she kept unwittingly walking into the creature, who had now re-appeared. I kept pushing her out of its way but things were certainly beginning to happen.

I managed to get Dianne back to bed and I knew I should not go back to sleep. As Dianne began to get sleepy the creature tried to attack her again. Dianne could not see what I was seeing, but she was aware of a very bad presence.

I now started to piece together the events of that evening and the reasons for the feeling I'd had when walking up the stairs earlier. I laid down on the bed and immediately watched a strange pattern appear upon the ceiling. I quickly picked up the paper and pencil that Dianne had left earlier by the bed, which I now believe had been clearly earmarked for me (this is often how things work out), and I proceeded to draw the pattern I was seeing. It was like a hand shape, with long fingers of different lengths. To the right of the picture I drew a small mass of scribbles. I did not tell anyone about this drawing for a while, until it became evident to me what it meant.

All through the night I felt the urge to keep going to the window. Neither Dianne nor I could sleep. The whole place, especially our bedroom, was disturbed. The large shimmering bear-like creature was frightened of me and I felt that I had the power to ward it off. Suddenly it appeared again. It realised it could not get me so it made a charge for Dianne. She felt its presence and screamed out, I threw myself across her, and this seemed to protect her. After a while I suggested to Dianne that we go downstairs and have some tea and get away from the bedroom. I guided Dianne down the stairs. As we came into the kitchen-dining room I instinctively knew where it was safe to sit, and where it was not. I knew that the house had a definite no-go area through it. There was a corridor coming in from outside the house which continued running through the cottage. The 'unsafe' corridor incorporated part of the kitchen-dining room and Mandy's bedroom. As we sat in the dining area drinking tea I started to work out what was happening. Something was entering, something bad and extraordinary. This was the reason why the phone and television had not worked that evening, why I had shivered on the stairs and why parts of the kitchen-dining room and our bedroom were effected. If the bed in our room had been moved slightly, Dianne's legs would have been outside of the 'unsafe corridor'. I now realised that I had been brought here for a definite purpose.

When we returned to bed we did not go back to sleep. I continued walking to and from the window. When the creature reappeared, I frightened it so much it flew at a great speed out of the window. I watched it fly higher at one point, as if going over something it wished to avoid. Once past that point, the creature returned again to its lower course, then shot off at speed across the valley's horizon, and out of sight. I asked Dianne if there was an oak tree outside the cottage. She replied that she had not noticed one. I found this odd as I could definitely see one shimmering. I went to the window again around 6:30 a.m. and called Dianne to come and look. The unsafe corridor starting from outside of the cottage was showing itself. Out in the fields were two lines of large black birds. One line sat on telephone wires, the other line on electricity wires. They faced each other sitting very still, they did not attempt to fly into the strange unsafe place. You may believe that this is normal behaviour for birds, but I can assure you this was very different; they were all sitting there just outside of the unsafe corridor for a purpose. It was as though they were confirming that this corridor was dangerous.

Some time passed and dawn came. We heard church bells, and looked down the valley to the church. I suddenly realised that this was why the creature soared up and over something in its retreat; the church was in its path and the creature did not like it.

We heard John and Isabel getting up so we went and met them on the landing. They were still both extremely drowsy. Isabel asked about the uproar during the night. I tried to explain but it was somewhat difficult, especially as I had since experienced some more unusual events, which I wanted to keep to myself at least for the time being.

We decided to leave the cottage but agreed to have some breakfast first and then pack. As we all went into the kitchen I knew that there would be some whistles in the room, one either side of the unsafe corridor. Without hesitation we all set about looking for them. I realised that the creature was frightened of loud high pitch noises, which was one of the reasons why I had made Dianne scream. I found one whistle on one side of the kitchen. Meanwhile, Isabel looked in a large pantry on the other side and found another. I had the distinct feeling these whistles had been used before.

After a light breakfast we all went into Mandy's bedroom. When we had first arrived, this room appeared to be lovely and warm. It was now freezing cold and we all felt very uncomfortable. I advised Dianne, John and Isabel to go and wait in the car. I stayed in the bedroom for a while and the presence appeared. With my full force I told it to leave Mandy, the cottage and the four of us for ever and never to return. I warned it that it did not belong here and had no

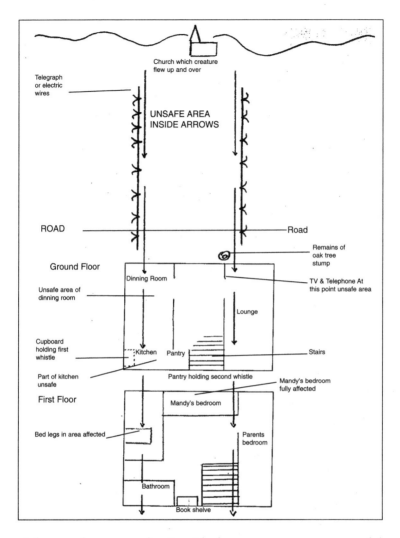

right to abuse people. I said there were more powerful things than it. The creature screamed and left.

I joined everyone in the car and told them what had just happened. We all agreed that we had better drive to Abergavenny and tell Dianne's parents about our experience; and to advise them that we were moving on, probably to visit John's relatives further into Wales. When we pulled into the campsite where Dianne's parents were staying, her mother was standing outside their caravan by the awning with outstretched arms as though she had been waiting for us. Dianne found this very strange, but immediately started to tell her mother all about our experiences. Doreen replied to Dianne, 'Yes I know. Do you remember that you and Isabel had been playing word games when you arrived at the cottage?' 'Yes', we replied. 'Well', said Doreen, 'the answer to solving this mystery will be found in the words'. Then Doreen and her husband, John, invited us into their caravan and they made some tea. John and Isabel fell sound asleep within moments of sitting down. It was all very odd. Anyway, we had our tea and left the in-laws and proceeded to John's relatives. John said that he would drive for the first part of the journey. We had only gone a few miles when Dianne, who was sitting in the back seat, caught a glimpse of John in the driver's mirror - he was falling asleep at the wheel. We got him to stop the car immediately and I took over the driving.

It turned out to be a lovely journey travelling across Wales. We reached John's relatives and spent the day with them. We found a lovely farmhouse to spend the night. It was comforting for us to be in such a lovely place with friendly people but, with all that had happened, Dianne was still terribly upset. She was too frightened to close her eyes in case the creature came again so hardly got any sleep. I tried to reassure her but to no avail. We all met up for break-fast and returned to John's family where we spent the day walking around the local village. It was very interesting as a mini-series for television was being made, and it helped us to take our minds off things for a while.

We thought we would leave reasonably early as we had quite a journey ahead of us, and we wanted to drive straight back home without too many stops. We were quite a way into our return journey when I suddenly had a strong piece of intuition. I told everyone that I would solve what had happened at the cottage before we crossed the Severn Bridge. Just as I said this I looked into my driver's mirror and saw five stars and a man's face. Then I remembered what my mother in-law had said; 'The answer is in the words'. I asked everyone if any words could be made from the letters in the village name Rhandimwyn. As I was driving I left it up to John, Dianne and Isabel to sort out. I advised them to look in the Road Atlas and see if there were five locations that looked of any significance around the village. The five places were to represent the five stars that I saw. They sorted out some places very easily but were clearly disturbed by what they had found. They had discovered two locations called Halfway, these were either side of the village. A third place was called Babel, the fourth Salem and the fifth place was a forest. I stopped the car in the nearest layby with some haste and fetched a piece of paper from the boot of the car.

This was the very same paper I had drawn upon in the bedroom at the cottage. It depicted the hand-like shape that I had seen on the ceiling but no one knew that I had drawn this. We got another piece of paper and Dianne and Isabel drew lines between the places that had been discovered by joining them together in a 'dot-to-dot' fashion, like in the children's game. The pattern which formed by joining these places up was exactly the same as the one I had previously drawn. Everyone was shocked when I presented them with my drawing. It was very eerie to see that they were both the same. Isabel and Dianne continued playing with the letters in the village name just as I had asked, suddenly they said 'Oh God'. They had realised that the words **'I Warn Mandy'** were within the name.

Earlier in this chapter I mentioned a piece of paper that Isabel and Dianne had found when they first played the cube-word game. This paper already had letters and numbers scribbled on it. At the time I did not know what

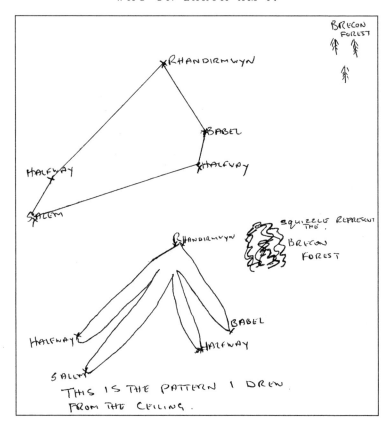

this meant, but I kept it anyway. Now, on checking the paper this is what we found:

The letters were written like this.

I=1   W=1   A=2   R=1   N=2   M=1   A=2   N=2
D=1   Y=1. (They were not originally in this order. I have put them like this for clarity).

These were all letters from the village name, the numbers show how many times they are needed in order to spell 'I warn Mandy'. Also written on the paper in red ink were the jumbled up letters of the names: Isabel, Dianne and Terry. For some reason John's name was not on it.

As bizarre as it seemed the clues to the puzzle were

becoming unjumbled and things were getting themselves sorted out.

We all sat in the car astonished. I shocked Dianne, Isabel and John even more when I pointed out that the village was situated between two locations called Halfway and a place called Babel, which according to the Bible is the stairway to heaven; and Salem which is connected with witchcraft and Satan. Therefore it appeared that we had been in a village halfway between heaven and hell!

It now became clear to me that someone near the cottage was involved in something untoward. I recalled that after Mandy had left hospital I was told that she needed something else to help her. Now I started to understand what it was. I had been sent to the cottage to discover what was going on. I am no stranger to these type of unusual happenings, it has occurred all my life. I am constantly put into these situations to sort things out.

We continued on our homeward journey but I did not feel completely safe. I made sure that I kept the piece of paper which had all our names written on it in my pocket. I needed to be sure of exactly where it was. I thought we were in some kind of danger. I knew from the way things happen in my life that, by keeping the paper in my possession, I would be able to control the situation.

We arrived home safely and although it was now getting late, I immediately rang Mandy's parents. I said we had stayed for two nights at the cottage and waited for a reaction. Mandy's mother responded with the famous phrase: 'Did you sleep all right?'. I told her we slept okay the first night but not the second and that we had received an unpleasant visitor, not of the human kind. Mandy's mother replied 'Oh', but did not seem shocked or surprised. She then explained that they had company, and said she would get her husband to telephone us when they had left.

It was a couple of days later when he did contact me. I briefly told him what had happened, and that I felt Mandy should not return to the cottage. Although sceptical, Mandy's father agreed and announced that he had put the cottage on the market.

As Dianne was still very distressed I rang our local vicar who is also a friend. I roughly explained the story from beginning to end, and he said he would come straight round. He spoke with Dianne for a little while and advised her of certain things she could do when she became frightened. The vicar said that this was not the first time that he'd had to deal with such things. He then said that he wanted me to meet someone very special, who was visiting the local church in the next few days. I went to the church as requested. The person he wanted me to meet was Robert Beatty the ex-Padre to the Queen, he was giving a talk on healing. After the meeting the Padre came straight up to me and asked me to visit him at one of his healing houses, where I could tell him the story about Wales. This man turned out to be a very important part of my life.

Approximately three weeks after the cottage episode I was out with Dianne at a large gathering. I felt that now it was okay to get rid of the paper which had our names on it. I screwed it up and asked the barmaid to throw it in the bin.

To date, the cottage has not sold and Mandy has had a slight relapse. I asked her mother when the relapse had occurred. She told me it had happened when she returned to the cottage which was about six months after we had left. I prayed for her and still do. I do not believe her parents ever told her about the events that took place in the cottage. I know that the Meningitis was caused by whatever was going on in the forest. Mandy's bedroom was one of the affected areas of the cottage.

The night we stayed in the cottage we were tricked into believing it would be nice. Far from it!

I came to the conclusion that when Mandy's parents stayed in the cottage and slept in their bedroom they were put into a state of deep sleep. This was why they would be unaware of what might be happening to Mandy. This is why John and Isabel were so tired after sleeping in that room.

Just out of interest: when we left the cottage I found the remains of a stump which would have come up outside Mandy's room. It was an oak tree which had been cut down. It was the one I saw through my mind 'shimmering'. Someone once told me that oak trees protect, they are guardians!

VERIFICATION

Isabel Mattick is a former Mayor of Bracknell and Borough Councillor. She and husband John are very highly respected by the local community. Her story of this incident runs for nine pages, and including the whole of it in this small book would not be practical. However, I have included some of the highlights from her account which corroborate my story:

'This is a true story. It could have happened to anyone - it still could.

'After doing our chores, we collected our cameras and decided to explore the village. As we strolled past the cottage next door, the neighbour, who had left the key, and looked after things when the family wasn't there, was in the garden. He asked if we had slept well. We walked towards the local Inn and stopped to view the hills on the other side of the valley, and took photographs of the cottage, or at least tried to - both cameras refused to co-operate.

'After we had eaten, Terry and John decided to watch television. Dianne and I decided not to and played some word games from the pile of boxed games belonging to the family. We made up some of our own rules for some games and followed the rule book for others. We didn't waste paper, just used the scraps used

by the family, and their words were quite distinctive in red felt tip ink.

'Mine and John's room was, the main bedroom. It was fully furnished and there were several Holy Bibles in the room, I thought perhaps the owners were Roman Catholics. The bed was comfortable and soon we fell asleep. Later that night, I was awakend by Terry asking if we were all right and had we heard Dianne screaming from a 'night-mare'? John was still fast asleep and I had heard nothing...

'Early the next morning it was perfectly obvious that something was seriously wrong. Dianne was very agitated and Terry refused to leave her side......I went down stairs by myself and went into the kitchen to make a cup of tea and to start breakfast. To get into the kitchen I had to climb some steps but, first, I had to move a chair out of the way to obtain access. In the kitchen I could hear the other three talking away and at no time did anyone else come in. I went to lay the table in the dining room at the foot of the steps, and again found my way blocked by the chair! It was not a rocking chair, it could not have moved by itself, and all the windows and doors were closed

'We took a good look around the cottage, and made a point of going into Mandy's bedroom. It seemed quite sunny and cheerful but, suddenly, we all felt it, the temperature dropped dramatically, and the hairs literally stood up on our necks and arms. Why? John who is naturally sceptical was affected as much as all of us. The room took on quite a different 'feel'; it was not a nice feeling. If we had not already decided to leave, we most certainly would have made our minds up then.

'....Terry drove back towards England and Dianne and I devoted the time to looking at the map and also at the scraps of paper on which we had played the word game. Various things began to fall into place. Even our game with the village name held a key, it *contained the words 'warn' and 'Mandy'. Mandy had to be warned to keep away from her cottage. All this, and it does seem unlikely, fitted into the jigsaw.*

'In Terry and Dianne's story you will remember the shape that appeared on the ceiling. Unknown to us all, Terry sketched it from memory almost straight away, and had put it into his luggage. He asked for the car key, and was back with us immediately; there was no time to draw it. Terry was sure that someone locally, perhaps in the village itself or surrounding area, was involved in some way.

'Dianne took her experience badly, and was very disturbed. Terry called in the local vicar who re-assured her that whatever the creature was, it had not followed us. Indeed we destroyed the piece of paper with the word games - we wanted no links. It took her a while to lose her fear.

'The story has not yet finished. There is more to come. Terry has lodged a statement with a local solicitor, saying what will happen. In due course that will be revealed.

'Dianne, has been married to Terry for many years, and also has a mother who is sensitive to a world that most of us cannot comprehend. On the other hand John and I had no previous experiences of this type. Although John was only affected by the atmosphere in Mandy's bedroom, and was a party to the drawing of the shape by identifying various places, he could appreciate all that happened. I had also never been involved in any other event such as this, but clearly was meant to be there and to experience some of the events.

'Dianne was Terry's weak spot, his achilles heel. Terry challenged the creature, it snarled at him, and in turn tried to get Dianne. We were lucky that Terry is such a strong character. What would have happened if he hadn't been there? Or would we have been

unaffected, because we were not a challenge to this fiendish creature.

'Who knows? But what John and I have learnt: Never accept that something can't happen, it can!'

CHAPTER 10

Voodoo

During the mid eighties, whilst in the local town, I met Roy, a neighbour of mine, he was suffering from Multiple Sclerosis. Previously he had used a wheelchair but now he was walking very awkwardly with two walking sticks.

Roy mentioned that there was something about me that made him feel better. We were only acquaintances but, on a couple of occasions, Roy had sat in my garden with me while his children had a swim in my pool. It might have been on these occasions that he felt I was doing him some good. Roy asked me if I could go to his home and see his wife, Kathy, who wasn't very well. I agreed to do this and after a few days I went to visit them.

I entered Roy and Kathy's home and sat in their lounge. Roy was a lot better by now, he had progressed from a wheelchair to two sticks. It must have taken me between ten and fifteen minutes when I suddenly realised that they had 'something' in their house that wasn't particularly nice; it was stopping me concentrating.

I said 'you have something upstairs that I think you should take out of the house'. Roy looked at his wife and said, 'I knew we shouldn't have that! Its under our bed, I'll go and put it in the garden'. He went upstairs and fetched it down, walked it through the hallway and straight out into the garden. I did not see what it was. The object was apparently given to him, it was Scandinavian. It might have been some sort of star which various healers had touched. I felt that maybe one of the people that had done so wasn't a very good person.

As soon as it was removed from the house I could concentrate. This caused a lot of excitement in the Orions who wanted to guide me in helping this family. In fact they were overpowering and it was a bit of a job containing them.

I sat holding Kathy's hand for a while. I felt that the Orions were giving her some healing. But it was obvious that she needed surgery for her condition. Kathy had a serious brain complaint. She was unable to move her eyes to look around at things. Kathy had to move her whole head in order to look in a different direction. This should not have happened according to the doctors, apparently if a female reached the age of sixteen this particular problem shouldn't occur. Kathy was thirty.

Due to the overwhelming excitement of my 'friends' I told Roy and Kathy I would have to leave but would return soon. There was something I had drawn at home on some paper which I wanted to show Roy. I thought it was very relevant to him.

I had been home about one hour when I received a call from Roy. He said that after I had left Kathy she became very tired and went to bed. There she had a strange dream. When Kathy woke she could move her eyes. This was lovely news.

I called back to the house a few days later with the picture I had drawn. At first Roy said it didn't mean anything to him. I told him he had worked abroad, that he had been in Africa dealing in something rare, but I wasn't sure what. Roy had set up a deal with a contact whereby the contact told Roy the whereabouts of the particular item he was looking for. The contact thought this deal was between Roy and himself and that Roy was paying him for the information. However it was Roy's company which was supposed to be paying.

I believe this is where things started to go wrong. I was getting this information through my psychic mind.

I told Roy he had been taken ill and hospitalised. The doctor didn't tell him what was wrong with him, and he appeared to be acting 'cagey'. I asked Roy if anyone had visited him whilst he was in hospital and if he could remember if the visitor had anything on their arm.

Roy was shocked and said 'Yes I had a visit from the man, the contact that gave the information'. Roy said that the man had a tattoo on his arm, which was the same as the picture I had drawn.

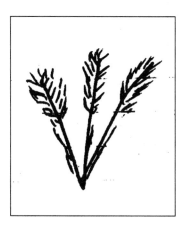

I asked Roy if the man had taken anything of his while he was there. Roy replied, 'Yes, my watch was missing'. I told Roy that I believed that this man also gave him something without his knowledge and whatever it was, it was in his home. I knew if he got 'rid of it', it would be the end of his troubles.

A spell or voodoo curse had been cast upon Roy for not paying this man, but the truth was, it was outside of Roy's control, the Company were meant to have paid.

The person with this power of voodoo can appear to cause harm without any consideration. Such power should not be used for trivial matters.

Roy was re-hospitalised in Germany and was told of his condition, Multiple Sclerosis. He obviously had to return home, where his condition worsened and he began to use mobility aids.

Kathy did go into hospital for complicated surgery but this story is not over.

Someday I feel that I should return to this house and complete some unfinished business.

Roy seems to be in good shape to date, he has no need for sticks. He is currently working with computers.

Stoby's Fish And Chip Restaurant

A few years ago I had a vision during the early hours of the morning. It was so strong that I thought I should draw what I was seeing. I drew a tall narrow building with some sort of mechanism on the top of it, which I knew to be a 'dumb waiter' this is a lift mechanism which usually transports food from a kitchen, on one floor, to a serving hatch on another level.

Next, I saw young children playing on top of this building. There was an area up there where you could walk around. These children, in sheer panic, frantically tried to get down and out of the building. The quickest route was for them to get into the 'dumb waiter' and lower themselves. This they did in a state of horror. The children were dressed in what I first thought was not the usual British clothing, and I wondered if this all might be happening in another country. Once the children had reached the entrance of the building I saw them run out into the street, and they were almost run over by what looked like an old bus. My wife watched me do the drawings. I told her what I had just experienced. We were both perplexed but managed to get back to sleep.

Two weeks later our friends, John and Isabel, the same couple who came with us when we went to Wales, asked if we fancied going out somewhere for the day. I had a friend who owned and ran a cafe in West Bay in Dorset. So I telephoned and advised him to expect us.

En route we stopped off at Yeovil to look around the Air Museum. We spent a couple of hours there. As we walked back to the car to continue our journey, Dianne said, 'Do you really want to go all the way down to West Bay?' We all felt the same, it was strange because we had all been looking forward to going there. Isabel asked, 'Where else shall we go, is there anywhere interesting locally?' Dianne replied, 'Let's go into Salisbury, we can look around, and get a meal somewhere'. We were all in agreement, although it did seem a rather odd choice as Salisbury was some distance and there were plenty of other cafes and restaurants nearby. However, Salisbury it was.

We arrived quite late to look around the shops, most had already closed. As we pulled into the town square we noticed a building with a banner strewn across it announcing some sort of exhibition inside. We found a parking place and looked to see if anywhere was open. We noticed a Woolworth store and, since it was 'late night Friday opening', we made for that. On the way we passed a restaurant, looked at the menu and decided on a nice steak. The restaurant didn't open for about three-quarters of an hour, so we thought that by the time we had browsed around the store, it would be just the right time to eat. After looking around, we were just about to leave Woolworth's when I said, 'I don't fancy steak after all', but somehow deep down I did, it was peculiar. Isabel said, 'Okay, shall we have some fish and chips?' We all agreed. Isabel asked the first passer-by if they could direct us to a fish restaurant and, as it happened, there was one just a short distance away.

As we entered the three storeyed building I charged straight up to the top floor, but suddenly realised that this floor wasn't for the general public, it was the staff offices. I went down a flight of stairs and met Dianne, John and Isabel coming up. We were now on the middle floor of the restaurant. The ground floor was a fish and chips take-away. We were shown in by a waitress and seated. Dianne picked up the menu and turned it over; on the back there was a short story about the building, Dianne remarked that apparently they had a ghost there. It had been heard on several occasions throughout the years. As Dianne said this I felt 'something' enter from behind me and urgently try to force me out of my chair. In my mind I told it to wait. I finished my meal but my body was shaking uncontrollably, everyone could see it. Meanwhile Dianne was staring in shock at the printed serviette. On it was a picture of the fish restaurant, the very same picture I had drawn two weeks previously. Dianne asked the waitress if the building had a 'dumb waiter'. She replied that it did have one up until 1981 when there had been a fire, and the building was re-furbished. Dianne probed the waitress about the ghost, she confirmed the story on the menu.

There was undoubtedly something strange happening. We quickly finished our meal. While I was paying, a date and a name came into my mind, it was George, a butcher. I asked Dianne and Isabel to go to the library and check the obituary column in all newspapers around the date I had given them; to see if anyone had died under unusual conditions. We were lucky - the library was open. This was the first building we noticed when we came into Salisbury, it was open late for the exhibition, so things were in our favour.

I arrived with John about ten minutes after Dianne and Isabel had entered the library. They were busy up to their eyes in microfiche. They said they were close to finding out what I had asked. They had discovered the death of a butcher called George whose premises were opposite the fish restaurant. Then the librarian asked them to clear up as she was closing in five minutes; they asked for more time, but to no avail. I was so frustrated that I stared at the librarian, and, as I did so she let out a shriek and said, 'God, I've got static running through me'. I believe this happened because of the way I looked at her, combined, possibly, with the 'force' I was trying to deal with; since we were so close to an answer to this riddle.

I said, 'Let's go back to the fish shop, I need to speak to the waitress again'. The waitress told me that they thought the ghost was a woman, I said it was a man. She then told me that a person many years ago, jumped off the top of the building and committed suicide. Very quickly I started piecing the puzzle together. I asked her if I could go to the top floor again; there was a reason. This appeared to be why I rushed up there in the first place.

I climbed the stairs on my own, leaving Dianne, John and Isabel on the second floor, but they could see me. When I entered the room, I watched an 'entity' rushing around and

A very rough sketch. Notice the three storeys, front door and window shape (Georgian frames). The mechanism on the top was the working for the 'dumb waiter'. I had drawn the restaurant as it was, pre-refurbishment!

around in a panic. It wanted to know who I was, I told him that he had suffered enough and that I was releasing him to go to a place of rest. With this he went. I told the waitress the ghost had gone and I had witnessed it go.

CONCLUSION

When I drew the picture two weeks previously, it was indeed this restaurant. Three children had been playing on top of the building, around the corner from where the man had jumped off. They witnessed him throwing himself off the building - he was their father! The man caught a glimpse of his children in a horrified state as he fell. So after his death he could not rest in peace. Everything was now coming through to me very clearly. I realised that the reason I thought the children might have been foreign, was due to the old fashioned clothes they were wearing. I said to John and Isabel, who were no strangers to peculiar 'happenings', 'When we get home, I'll show you the pictures I drew of this place'. They couldn't wait - spooky but true!

CHAPTER 12

The Snake

A year after my back operation I purchased my first home in Bracknell, Berkshire. A Doctor and his wife lived next door and we became good friends. The Doctor knew that at the time I was working at a large lawnmower centre, and that sometimes I serviced my family's mowers at my home. One day he asked if I had a large mower that might cut an elderly gentleman's lawn. An old chap lived in a property a little further down the road and was incapable of doing it himself. The Doctor asked me if I would cut the grass free of charge for the gentleman. Without hesitation I replied, 'Of course, that goes without saying'.

Later that afternoon I loaded a lawnmower into my car and drove to the old gentleman's chalet bungalow. The lawn was extremely overgrown and it presented a bit of a challenge. However, I started mowing but after a short while the mower struck an object. It was a gravestone and, for some reason, I felt really uncomfortable. I didn't like the old chap's bungalow - full stop, let alone without coming across this! My instincts told me to pack up and go back home. My wife looked at me, surprised that I had returned so soon. I told her what had happened. It was a shame that I had to abandon the gentleman's lawn, and I felt rather uneasy about telling the Doctor why I had stopped. After all, I was a 'grown man' and I looked a bit of a wimp being scared off by a grave; but there was much more to it than just that. The whole premises gave me a bad feeling, and every time I drove past the bungalow I would see a lady's face peering out of the top bedroom window. I always felt compelled to look up at it. After this incident was over, apart from still looking up at the window whenever I passed by, I got on with my life.

Going ahead in time - to the mid-eighties. I met up with some friends who had recently purchased this very same chalet bungalow. It had been sold once before, so my friends, Iain and Jenny were the second owners since the elderly gentleman. Iain, was a Bracknell Borough Councillor while I was a Town Councillor, so we obviously met on several occasions, both socially and through council meetings. As a result my wife and I became very good friends with them.

At a fund raising event one evening, another councillor-friend was speaking to Jenny about a strange experience which happened when she and her husband had been on holiday with Dianne and I. Jenny must have thought a lot about what she had heard, because shortly after this particular evening she telephoned and invited Dianne and I to spend an evening with her and Iain. We got together and during our conversation she asked me, if I could feel if anything wasn't quite right with the house. At the time nothing felt wrong but as we were leaving and saying our goodbyes in the hallway, I sensed something. I told Jenny that I would come to see her in a couple of days.

Two days later I returned. Jenny and I chatted in her lounge, then I said, 'Let's look around'. We went upstairs and both felt drawn to the eldest daughter, Claire's bedroom. Jenny said she always felt a presence there. There was a little doorway in this room leading into the eaves, both Jenny and I felt something in there. I had to lure it out. Suddenly, Jenny witnessed an 'entity' engulfing me and she watched me bring it down the stairs as I was saying, 'We are going down. Come with us'. When we reached the lounge Jenny said, 'I can see a blue haze all above you'. She looked very concerned for me. Then all of a sudden the 'entity' took the form of a snake. It shot away at great speed retreating through the garden door, causing something like a huge vacuum as it left. Jenny agreed that it felt like the air had been sucked away. She described me as looking 'grey and very fatigued', and I must admit that after this experience, that is exactly how I felt.

Jenny proceeded to tell me what had started to happen shortly after they had purchased the house. Jenny had two teenage daughters, Kirstin and Claire. They were often alone in the house as Iain had to work abroad sometimes for long spells, returning only for brief periods. Jenny told me that it wasn't unusual to feel uneasy whilst alone in bed. The bedroom featured a floor to ceiling window and, on one particular night, Jenny felt more uneasy than ever before. She did, however, eventually 'doze' off. Jenny dreamt of a snake slithering outside her window, it slithered up and came inside. Still slithering it came across the floor and up on to the bed. The snake appeared to have three heads. She woke, absolutely terrified and jumped out of bed, almost throwing herself into the hall. Jenny frantically put the hall lights on and sat down on the carpet. Then strangely, as quickly as the terror had engulfed her, it went. Jenny returned to bed without even looking around. She told me that she could not believe how peaceful she felt. That being so, she went straight back to sleep.

Jenny said that at the time this occurred the property was undergoing major alterations. The most important job was having the blue asbestos removed from the loft area. It was causing chaos. Jenny described the men who arrived to do the work as looking like 'spacemen', since they were dressed in similar fashioned clothing, complete with hoods, etc. A triple tunnel was set up, which involved three air-locking compartments, they had to pass through each one to stop the risk of contamination. The 'spacemen' walked to and from these chambers locking each one whilst carrying out the removal work. They came for five days, working from ten in the morning until three in the afternoon; the disruption was enormous. Apparently the tunnels went right up inside the eaves. Jenny pointed out the point of entry to the loft and eaves, which was through the doorway in Claire's bedroom.

After the snake incident Jenny was very fearful when Iain announced that he had to go abroad again. She really didn't want him to leave and got herself very worked up, so that eventually she gave herself severe stomach pains. However, Iain had to go. It was shortly after Iain had left that Jenny retired to bed. She had just gone off to sleep when she had a nightmare of a huge spider. Jenny is petrified of spiders, and worst still, the spider appeared to have a woman's face, and was hanging over her. The legs were hairy and she felt the spider sucking and draining energy from her body. Eventually she awoke from the horrible dream.

A couple of weeks passed after this awful incident and then a more frightening one occurred. Iain's mother was now living with them, she also saw the following incident:

Jenny was child-minding a baby girl called Abigail, who was happily playing in the very spacious hallway. To ensure that Abigail could play safely, Jenny had put a kitchen bench across the doorway between the kitchen and the hall. This stopped Abigail from crawling into the kitchen where she could touch things and hurt herself. Jenny was sitting straddled across the bench in the doorway, so she could keep an eye on the baby, as well as being able to talk to her mother-in-law, who was sitting at the kitchen table on the other bench. This bench was situated so that her mother-in-law's back was facing the sink.

They were chatting away to each other when Jenny said that she felt someone staring at her from behind, suddenly she heard a tremendous swishing noise. She described it like 'someone sucking in air'. At the same time as she heard this noise she sensed that whatever was behind her was also making a sound like a huge heartbeat; almost like a thump in the chest. Then, in her mind's eye, she watched an entity come down the stairs. The entity then hit her in the back with full force. So powerful was the blow that it forced her up off the bench and across the kitchen floor, lifting her up to the height of the sink where she hit her stomach. Her mother-in-law could not believe what she had seen. The distance Jenny was thrown must have been at least five to six feet.

The mother-in-law now refers to this incident as, 'the time Jenny flew!' After they got over the initial shock, the entity went away. Jenny's next thought was for the baby, she rushed over to see if Abigail was all right. Fortunately she was fine, happily playing, oblivious to what had just happened - thank goodness! Apparently Jenny had seen 'ghosts' ever since she had first moved in, especially in her bedroom. These bedroom visitors were nice, not threatening at all. Jenny said that when they appeared to her they looked like 'stardust', they sparkled all around the room, comforting her. She said that the entities in her home appeared to be a mixture of good and bad sources, and were at war with each other.

To sum up the story: after speaking to Iain and Jenny, I managed to get rid of the entity. Iain seems to think, and I agree, that the interference in the loft somehow disturbed something bad in there, which caused part of the problem. All has remained well in the household to the present day. It is in fact a lovely warm family home and very peaceful. As I pass the bungalow now it looks very nice. The woman at the window, of course, disappeared!

Iain was very sceptical at first, he finds the nature of the paranormal hard to accept. He is a very straightforward, intelligent, good man. So I felt I needed to tell Iain something, in order that he might have confidence in me. I told him that when he was a child he had a toy clown called 'Coco', and I said 'You pulled its leg off didn't you?' Ian replied, 'Wow!' I told him other things to do with his family, but that's another story!

CHAPTER 13

Shopping in Windsor

M y wife wanted to buy a new jacket, so we decided to go to Windsor. I thought it would be nice to have a stroll around afterwards; there is quite a lot to do there and it is only fifteen minutes away from our home.

When we arrived I made a bee-line for the end part of the town. Dianne said, 'Don't go that way, I don't think there are any clothes shops down there'. I knew she was right, the main shops were up by the castle, but I wanted to go in the other direction. Dianne followed but she wasn't happy.

I said to Dianne, 'Daniel'. She replied 'What do you mean, are you talking about, Daniels the department store? If so, you are going the wrong way'. I said, 'No, just Daniel'. I wasn't sure myself why I had said that. Anyway we walked a little way and finally came across a ladies' clothes shop; quite a large one in fact. After Dianne chose a jacket she liked, the manageress came over to her and asked if she would like to try on one of their new dresses which had only came that day. Dianne said, 'Yes'. She picked one out and looked for a changing room, there were quite a few to choose from. Dianne said 'I think I'll go into this one it's nice and big'. The manageress said 'There is a door in that cubicle, it leads down to the road'. Dianne for a joke said, 'Oh, that's good, if I like the dress I can slip out without paying'. The manageress replied, 'You won't want to go down there, there is a ghost!' Dianne said to herself, 'Here we go again'.

The manageress asked her what she meant. Dianne replied, 'It's a long story but strange things happen when Terry is around'. The lady looked puzzled. 'Don't worry', said Dianne 'it's usually all for the good, perhaps someone needs healing or help'. Consequently the manageress said to

111

me 'Would you like to go down and have a look around?' I replied, 'I don't mind'. I asked her if she wanted to come down with me, she said, 'Oh no!' However the shop assistant said, 'Can I go down there?' The manageress replied, 'Yes, if you want to'. The young lady and I went down the stairs leading off from the cubicle; immediately I saw the ghost of a man hanging from a rope, his feet dangling off the ground. I could see that the original floor level had been lower at the time of his death but was now higher. I said to the young lady, 'You can talk to it if you like, it is harmless'. She replied, 'No, I'm too frightened to'. We stayed for a moment then went back upstairs.

In the meantime Dianne had told the manageress about the healing that occurs when I am around people. Consequently, the instant I returned, she said, 'I would like to go down there after all'. So down we went. As we stood there I looked at the ghost, and I received a spiritual message from him. I relayed the information to the manageress: I told her that she had a daughter called Elizabeth who had a young son called Daniel and that Daniel had some ear trouble and had recently been in hospital. The manageress was extremely shocked, she replied, 'Yes, I do have a daughter called Elizabeth, and a grandson Daniel; he has been unwell; and only recently he had an operation to put some grommets into his ears'. Then she said, 'What shall I do, what's happening?' I said, 'Don't worry, the ghost is nice. When you see Daniel next time, kiss him all around his ears and he will be fine'.

I was also told 'spiritually', that the manageress had just received a bunch of flowers. When I told her this, she replied that a customer had recently given her some, but I said, 'No, your husband has given you a bunch'. 'Oh', she replied, 'that's right, he wants a reconciliation with me. He is coming around at the weekend for a decision'. I told her that I thought she should have him back; he would be good for her, and she would need him in the future. The manageress replied, 'Well, I'm seriously thinking about it'.

We returned up the stairs. The manageress was very excited. She said to my wife and the shop assistant, 'You will never believe what this man has said to me. He has mentioned my daughter, my grandson and husband!'

I told them that the ghost had a friend in a nearby pub, who had also hanged himself. After this I said that we had better go. The manageress packed our shopping and I paid her. Just before we left, she asked if I would call in and see her again and I replied that I would. Once outside the building I said to Dianne I had felt drawn to that shop. The name Daniel was the lady's grandson, he had probably needed a little 'extra help'; and had been nothing to do with the shop with the same name in Windsor High Street.

A week after this incident some friends of mine, Justin and Jane, who lived in London, asked if they could come and stay for the weekend. I said, 'Of course'. They came down and we had a good day together. As the evening came we were wondering what to do. Justin said, 'Have you had any ghostly things happen recently?' So I began to tell them about Windsor. Jane and Justin said, 'Can we visit the pub, where the other ghost is and see what happens?' Well, I don't particularly go looking for things, but I thought, 'Oh well, what the hell, why not?'

We all set off for Windsor. I parked down by the river Thames. After a short stroll we made for the turning where the clothes shop and pub were. I pointed the pub out to Justin, I knew the second ghost was there. As we approached the pub we could see that it was shut. On the door there was a sign saying that it was closed for refurbishment. Jane and Justin were a little disappointed, but I told them not to worry. Jane was standing almost on top of where the ghost was below in the pub cellar. I said to Jane, 'Stay still, I'm picking up things from him'. Justin said that he felt very cold and thought he could feel a presence. Jane had been a long-time sufferer of arthritic knees. I felt that the ghost was going to help her get some relief. I relayed this message to Jane. Then I said that for some strange reason, she should put her hands in amongst a large quantity of frogs! She would find them after taking a ride on a green bus. This all seemed very odd to Justin and Jane, but they had witnessed strange events with me in the past, so they took it all in their stride, and said they would wait and see what turned up.

The following weekend I received a phone call from Justin. He said, 'You'll never guess what happened today. Jane and I decided to get a bus to visit a shopping mall in Croydon. The buses here are not normally green, but the one that came along was'. Justin said, 'I didn't start putting two and two together until we went inside the mall. Just inside the entrance was a very large container and in it were hundreds of little green soft toy frogs. Jane immediately pushed her hands in amongst them'. I told Justin that I believed it was because Jane was very fond of soft toys, she was comforted by them. Consequently she received a psychological form of healing. Jane got a lot better, she was able to reduce her tablets for arthritis, to the bare minimum. I don't always understand the unusual ways of healing, I just know to believe them.

These are just two, of many, ghostly occurrences. It would take so long to write about them all. I have written about these events particularly, as they can be authenticated. Other experiences, some quite frightening for those involved, cannot be mentioned, because the people concerned, do not wish it to be made public.

The Ghostly Cat

I have a great respect for cats, they are extremely clever and cunning. I personally believe that they come from the planet Sirius, and were used partly for the manufacture of mankind. I think that certain breeds of cats probably have similar DNA in their blood to that of the early Pharaohs. If people come to me with a cat problem of a ghostly nature, I like to investigate.

In 1993, Mark, the nephew of my best friend Dave Bellhouse, was experiencing a rather bad time. Mark was living at home with his mother in a small terraced house in London. Dave came to see me and said that Mark was screaming at night from a recurring nightmare. On a couple of occasions he had screamed so loudly that the neighbour had heard him. Mark thought that there might be mice or rats under the floorboards in his bedroom, because he constantly heard scratching. David was getting very concerned, particularly after one night when Mark awoke from a nightmare screaming and some scratches appeared on his shoulder.

Dave took up Mark's floorboards and did a thorough inspection, but he couldn't find any evidence of rats or mice; there were no droppings or litter: no clues at all. Dave invited me to his nephew's house to see if I could help.

I went to the house and spoke to Mark about the nightmares and the strange things that had been happening. After a little while I went to their toilet. There I saw a large domestic cat, not living, but a huge ghostly one. I came out and Sue, Mark's mother, approached me and said 'Have we got anything in the house?' I said that I had just seen a cat in the toilet, she replied, 'I haven't got any cats, I'm petrified of them'. I felt that I should go into Mark's bedroom, which was on the ground floor. As I crossed the hallway the same cat reappeared, sprang up, leapt over my shoulder and shot up the stairs.

I told Mark that the cat had just gone upstairs. I said 'Are you coming up to find it?' I had in my possession a Bible which Robert Beatty the ex-Padre to the Queen had given me - a special one. It had been all around the world helping with healing. We went into Mark's mother's room and I could hear the cat scratching behind the bricks in the chimney breast. It was an old house which still retained a bedroom fireplace. The ghostly cat was hiding in a cavity in the brickwork. I persuaded it to leave the house and the family alone.

I believe that Mark had conjured up the cat during his investigations into ancient magic. After this visit all paranormal activity ceased. Mark's arm which had persistently bothered him presented no further problem.

Unusual Activity

Another incident involving telepathy occurred between me and my grandson who is also psychically gifted. We were together with some friends at a pub restaurant called 'The Barge' in Alton Barnes, Wiltshire. I was introduced by some friends to a husband and wife. My grandson looked at the husband and said to me. 'Grandad, that man has his dead brother in him'. I tried to keep him quiet in case the man overheard. I was reluctant to chastise Barry, because I've been with him when many strange things have occurred. Anyway it just so happened that this particular man, who I'll call Bob, entered into conversation with me. Bob went on to say that he was having problems; weird things were happening to him, and he was very depressed since the suicide of his brother. He was finding it very hard to do his job at work. Bob said that people were picking on him. After a couple of weeks I decided to invite Bob and his wife to my home. They were a nice couple, we spoke for hours, I think it was helpful. We left it that he would contact me soon with an update, and possibly meet at his home.

I did not hear back from Bob until nearly a week later. Apparently he had trouble with his car after he left my house. One of his rear lights and indicators was not working. Bob had left my house when it was dark, and motorists tooting their horns warned him of the problem. The curious thing was, that my car also received damage to the rear that evening. When I told Bob and his wife, I think they thought that Dianne had driven into their car sometime during the day. We later found out that the damage caused to my car happened when it was parked at the local supermarket and subsequently the manager accepted full liability.

At the time I still felt that this couple were unconvinced,

so I suggested that I drive my car over to them, so that they could see whether the damage to my vehicle corresponded to the damage on theirs. This I did and when Bob saw it, he agreed that in no way could my car have been responsible for the damage to his - it didn't even match up. However, it is still a mystery as to how Bob's car got damaged. Perhaps it involved some sort of paranormal incident?

Whatever happened, this incident led me to visit Bob's home, which was a good thing because whilst I was there, he said to me, 'I was on my computer when a lot of dots came up on the screen. I don't understand what it is or what it means'. Fortunately Bob had printed out what he had seen. I replied that he should go and fetch it and let me look, so he went upstairs and brought the piece of paper down. I said 'Where is the other piece?' He said 'Oh, I've screwed it up, it's in the bin, what do you want that for?' I replied, 'You'll see'.

Bob went and retrieved the other piece of paper and smoothed it out. When he handed it to me I turned it upside down and placed it on top of the first piece. I then told him to switch his television on but keep the sound down. He looked at me inquisitively. I placed the papers in the same position against the screen. The light from the screen shone through the papers revealing a photo picture of Bob's dead brother. Bob was really shocked, he asked me what he was supposed to do. I suggested that Bob should go to the place where his brother had committed suicide and ask him to leave him alone. His brother's life was over, but Bob's wasn't. I told Bob that he should tell his brother that he must stop trying to rule his life. I asked Bob if he had any pictures of him, and if he hadn't, he should get some and put them around the home in order to give his brother a little attention.

I called Bob after a month and he was feeling better. I've not contacted him since so I hope things work out for him. One thing though - my grandson was perfectly right!

CHAPTER 16

Jersey

My mother's family came from Jersey, hence my Jersey middle name, 'Le Riche'. A large number of shopping stores are run in Jersey by the Le Riches. I always wanted to visit the island but never seemed to get around to going there. This was to change in May 1993, when I finally made the trip. My wife and I had a lovely break, the island was beautiful, but it wasn't without its mystery. I had two strange encounters. One of which had quite an impact on me.

It was our last day in Jersey, we were driving around trying to fill the time before our flight home. After visiting a carnation factory, I called in on a museum at L'Oeillère. It was only a small place, a converted bunker on the coast. The bunker had been used by the Germans whilst they occupied the island during the war. It was filled with memorabilia, and there was a story about a plane crew that had been shot down from this very bunker.

As I walked around through the first part of the bunker I heard a man's voice speaking to me. It said 'They haven't got it right'. I looked around, but nobody was there. I rushed to tell my wife, who wasn't too interested in the museum and was already halfway round the place. I told her what had just happened, and she looked at me as if to say, 'Oh dear! here we go again'. Suddenly a lady (not a ghost) came running up to me, grabbing my arm and pulling me towards a friend she was with. Then she said, 'I don't know why I am doing this, I don't know you but I want you to meet this gentleman, his name is Leonard'.

Leonard was standing next to a plaque on the wall. It displayed information and pictures all about him. 'Leonard', I said, 'before you say anything come with me'. I took him into the place where I had heard the voice. I said, 'Can you hear anybody talking'. 'No', he replied. I then proceeded to tell him:

'It's wartime, you are in your plane with your crew on a bombing mission. The bombs are dropped, but not in the right place, but it doesn't matter, it didn't do any harm. You are not sure what islands you are over. It's very cloudy and you are low on fuel. You pull something behind you, then the plane lowers to look under the clouds. You then realise that they are the Channel Islands. The plane is spotted and shot down from this bunker. The plane crashed into the sea, but for some reason the Germans stopped firing, possibly they thought that the crash would kill you all anyway. One person with an odd nickname, I think you call him 'Brahm', is with another crew member struggling to get into a dinghy. The dinghy will not inflate. You think they will be all right because they had life jackets on, so you swim off. Unfortunately your friend Brahm drowned. Well, what Brahm is saying, through me to you, is that you shouldn't blame yourself for his drowning, you didn't know that he couldn't swim'.

Leonard, now in his seventies became very emotional. I said, 'I'm sorry, I didn't mean to upset you'. He replied, 'I didn't know he couldn't swim'. I asked Leonard to come to the top of the bunker, we looked out to sea. I could see through my mind all that happened to that fated crew all those years ago. I told Leonard that when the plane crashed the pilot survived but the navigator did not live, he was still in the plane. I pointed to an approximate area in the sea where the plane was to be found. Leonard looked at me and said, 'Yes all that did happen. I did pull something behind me in the plane, it was for reserve fuel'.

Damien, the person who looked after the museum, said, 'Don't let the Portuguese workers hear you talk about ghosts, or they won't work here'. I also told Leonard that the German who had shot them down got reprimanded for not continuing to fire on them, and that they were taken as

'Prisoners of War'.

We all decided to go to a nearby cafe and have a cup of tea. Leonard wanted to spend some time with us, but I had to catch my plane. We were quite bewildered by the event. Leonard asked for my telephone number and said that he had always been very distressed by his friend's death, it was something that he couldn't forget.

Apparently Leonard had visited the bunker the previous year. He read the plaque on the wall and knew that the story was wrong. So he told the curator in order to rectify this. He returned that following year to ensure that the plaque was properly corrected.

Leonard's lady friend, Barbara, was completely beside herself, she thanked me for what had happened, although she admitted that she didn't know what came over her, grabbing me in the way that she did. It appeared that once again, I was in the right place at the right time - coincidence? I wonder!

I received a telephone call from Leonard about six weeks after returning home from Jersey. Leonard had taken time to reflect on what had happened that day in the bunker. He said that he had just plucked up courage to telephone me and say, 'Thank you'. Leonard had been able to sleep now without thinking about his friend. He said that not a day had passed by without him thinking of me. I said to Leonard, 'By the way, your friend's full name was Abraham wasn't it? And you called him Brahm for short'. He replied, 'Yes, that's right'. I told Leonard that Abraham had an idea that he was going to die before the fated mission.

Just before we said our goodbyes, I told him that whilst he was in Jersey, just after I had left, his friend Barbara went on a boat trip and befriended a man. The man asked Barbara for her telephone number and said that he would be in touch with her. I said that the man had not contacted her. Leonard replied, 'Yes, that did happen, and no, he didn't get in touch with Barbara'.

I contacted the Jersey Museum recently to ask if they could send me any information about the bombing incident with Leonard Bolke. The person who runs the museum, Ian, remembered me visiting there that day. He was very helpful and sent me lots of information including photocopies of all the crew members. When I looked at the photos of Abraham it was very strange to think that this was the person I had communicated with that day. Ian told me that since I had been there strange things have happened. He said that his wife had been doing some bookwork there, late one night, when what seemed like a teardrop landed on her lap, but the ceiling was dry.

On another occasion, Ian was showing visitors around when groaning noises came out from the walls, no one could explain what they were.

VERIFICATION

'I was named after my father - Leonard Charles Bolke. I was eighteen when the war started in 1939 and knowing that I would be called up for military service of some sort, I decided to volunteer for the RAF which I preferred to the Army or Navy.

'It was summer of 1942 before I finished my Air Gunner's course and went to Operational Training Unit. This is where the crews were brought together for training units. It was thought to be better if the crews got together themselves rather than being directed.

'After the crews had made themselves complete, we were all called together one morning and told that there were two men left over from an earlier course, and it was decided that all the pilots names were to be put into a hat and picked out to decide the crew for these two people.

'Our pilot's name was drawn out twice, so we had the two peo-

*ple concerned, whom we had not yet met. This meant that we
exchanged a navigator and rear gunner in this manner. This
proved to be a lottery with fatal results, as it will be seen later in
this story.*

'*When on holiday in October 1990, I visited the War History
Museum in the German Bunker at St. Queens Bay, Jersey. There I
met Mr. and Mrs. Ian Cabot. Our combined interest and enthusi-
asm has brought about my attempt to tell the full story behind
the report that an* RAF *bomber came down into the sea early on
the 11th April 1943.*

'*The members of the crew were as follows:*

PILOT   Sgt W E Scott RAF *Bristol* Age 22

NAVIGATOR Sgt A Holden RAF *Accrington* Age 22

BOMB AIMER Sgt E A Odling RAF *London* Age 22

WIRELESS OP' Sgt L C Bolke RAF *Manchester* Age 22

REAR GUNNER Sgt G A Booth RCAF *Ottawa, Canada* Age 30

'*We were flying a Wellington Mark* X HE 213 F *from squadron,
Royal Canada Airforce,* NO 6 *group bomber command, based at
Burn, near Selby in Yorkshire.*

'*Up to date, we had bombed various targets in the Rhur, Keil and
Hamburg, as well as laying mines in the shipping lanes off the
Dutch coast. For this last, and for some of us, fatal mission we
were briefed to bomb Frankfurt on Maine.*

'*As this was beyond our normal range, we had fitted an overload
petrol tank in the bomb bag, and carried a mixture of high
explosives and incendiary bombs to complete the load. This
reduced our effective bomb load by half. Because of our limited
range we routed to return to Tangmere in Sussex instead of our
base in Yorkshire.*

'Records tell that we took off at 23.22 hours on 10th April 1943. I remember that we routed to avoid Amsterdam and the heavily defended Ruhr. We were to look for white track markers and adjusted course for this target area. On arrival, we found heavy opposition from search lights and flak, plus complete cloud cover several thousand feet below our bombing height of 18,000 feet. There were no bombing markers being dropped by the pathfinder aircraft. Somewhat confused, we circled this heavily defended area for some twenty minutes and still saw no markers.

'It was decided that we could not afford to waste any more fuel, so we made a bombing run through the heaviest flak and bombed the area. We were not aware of being hit at that point, and the navigator gave the pilot a course to steer for the return leg. This should have taken us on a straight track south of Saarbrucken to about Rheims. A dog leg adjustment to our course should have been made to avoid Paris, we then would cross the coast near Dieppe and continue onto our landing in Sussex. However with cloud cover still complete we could see nothing on the ground other than odds bits of flak from time to time.

'We seemed to have been flying for a long time. I checked the main fuel tanks which by this time were very low. I reported this to the pilot. It was my job to bring on the last petrol supply into the two engine nacelles. To do this I stood with both arms extended sideways, grasping a wire toggle in each hand, and when the engines started to falter, I pulled the toggles: we were now using our last twenty minutes supply of petrol.

'The pilot asked me to get a fix by radio, which I questioned as a risk if we were still over enemy territory. Skipper decided to go down and have a look, we entered cloud at thirteen thousand feet, and came out at three thousand. We saw the coast, and I was transmitting to get a fix, when islands were seen.

124

'Very accurate, heavy flak, got us immediately, and continued.
The skipper gave the order 'Prepare to Ditch' and I changed my
signal to 'SOS Ditching'. We all acknowledged the order except
the Rear Gunner - George Booth. The Skipper called to him, 'Did
you get that? We are ditching'. His reply, very brusquely was 'I
got it - Okay God dammit' and we never heard another word
from him. I believe he was badly wounded.

'When the trailing aerial touched the sea and cut my signal, I told
the Skipper we were down to fifty feet then switched over to my
fixed aerial on top of the aircraft so that having clamped down
my Morse key, a signal would continue until it sunk. (SOS was
received at 06.08).

'Now in my crash position, I waited for the crash landing, which
was perfectly done using the technique of lifting the nose at the
last moment so that the tail hits the water first and then settles
with the next bump or so. After the first bump I moved towards
the exit position, we hit the water again and I was thrown
around the aircraft 'like a pea in a bucket'. When I had picked
myself up, I struggled along to the escape hatch and with some
difficulty climbed out. The fuselage was burning from midship to

tail and belts of ammunition to the tail turret were on fire and exploding, the port engine was burning from when we were first hit.

'As I got out, I saw that two men were at the partly inflated dinghy and I dived into help, it was hopeless and we had to abandon it when the wrecked aircraft sank. I struggled to get rid of my parachute harness, inflate my life jacket, and started to swim towards the island in view. There were three of us, but I was not sure who was with us besides the pilot. I must have lost consciousness and have no memory of how long we were swimming or what sort of boat picked us up.

'I awoke to see German soldiers around my bed in a hospital ward on the upper floor. One soldier said in English 'For you the war is over.

'My leg was x-rayed and put into plaster, and a man from the Red Cross, Dr Shone, called and promised to send news to our next of kin that we were alive and had been taken as Prisoners of War.'

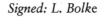

Signed: L. Bolke

'Brahm' - Sgt A Holden

CHAPTER 17

King's Cross Fire

I t was the day of the horrific fire at King's Cross Station, it was approaching late afternoon. I was getting ready to go to a local country club called 'Lakeside' in Frimley Green, Surrey. Dianne and her parents were also going, so I was looking forward to a nice relaxing evening. We arrived at about six o'clock in order to get an early meal and good seats to enjoy the show. Our meals were brought to us and everyone tucked in. At this point I didn't feel very much like eating. I was just playing with my food. I felt troubled about something, but I hadn't a clue as to what. The evening progressed, we were entertained by several acts. My mother-in-law looked at me and asked what was wrong, she had noticed that I had been very distant and subdued for hours. I apologised for being unsociable, I hadn't realised that I had been quite so inward.

It was soon approaching 1 a.m. and the show was coming to a close, so we gathered up our things and left to go home. Feeling extremely tired and troubled I got into bed about 2.15 a.m. It didn't seem long after this that I sat up in bed and said to Dianne, 'It's no good I'm burning up, I feel like I'm on fire, I cannot breathe, I'm choking!' The choking was the worst. I felt so awful. I said to Dianne, 'I can't cope with this, I've unloaded some of it onto Angela'. Angela is my youngest daughter, she was sixteen at the time. I was sorry for doing this, I really didn't mean for this to happen. I said to Dianne, 'Any minute now she will wake up'. This she did. Angela screamed for us to come into her bedroom. Before we could get up, Angela beat us to it, and jumped into the middle of our bed. I think the last time she did that was when she was about ten years old. Angela said, 'Dad, I'm sweating ... I'm so hot ... I can't breathe properly ... I feel like I'm choking!'. I knew this was going to happen. I tried to calm her explaining that I also felt this way and that we would try and sort it out. We all talked it over for some time.

Angela said that when she was in her bedroom she'd had a nightmare. She watched a mug floating above the pouffé which was on the floor, and every time she tried to grab the mug it floated further away. I asked Angela to describe the mug. She said that it was white with a lion figure on it, the lion was a maroon colour with gold edging around it. Angela was extremely upset and sweating. Dianne and I talked it over trying to make sense of everything. Furthermore, I said that I could see a white van driving to and fro to Scotland and also a small earthquake. After that, I don't think we really managed to get back to sleep properly.

It must have been about 6 a.m. when I switched the television on in our bedroom. There it was. A tragedy had taken place. There had been a terrible underground fire at King's Cross Railway Station, people were dead, others were badly burned; there was carnage everywhere. The television coverage of the scene with the ambulances, fire crew and the injured, was haunting. All three of us sat up in bed and knew that this was what I had seen in my mind and went through that night.

My son, Christopher, joined us in our bedroom when he heard the commotion. I said to Angela, 'That mug you described, that's the mug you got when you went to the Queen's Jubilee street party in 1977. The lion is the crest'. Dianne ran to the kitchen cupboard to fetch it and showed it to her, 'Yes', Angela said, 'that's the mug I saw last night'. I knew that Angela had picked up some sort of vibes, a connection relating to the Jubilee mug. Many people changed trains at the Jubilee underground station that night. Those heading for King's Cross totally unaware of their fate as no warning could be given. The fire started at around seven o'clock that evening, because we left the house earlier I had no knowledge of the tragedy, only that something bad was happening.

If I had not been so tired when I arrived home from the Country Club I probably might have switched the television on, and prevented a torturous night for us all. I was still thinking about the white van and wondering where this fitted in, when a news report revealed a story about a person picking up plasma in a white van from Scotland. So much plasma had been needed for the burn victims that the hospitals in the South were running out. In one way I was relieved because I had just rung a family friend, Sheila, to enquire if her son, Gordon, was okay; I knew that he was driving a white van at the time going about his business in Scotland.

Christopher made a cup of tea and said, 'That's it, I'm off to work to get away from these 'Ninja's', as he called them. This is the word he uses for want of a better one referring to my 'contacts'. Angela didn't go to school that morning, we were all quite worn out and shocked.

A few hours passed and then Christopher came home. This was most unusual, he rarely came home for lunch. I looked at his face and said, 'Go on, what's up?' He replied, 'You are not going to believe this. I was working at a lady's house doing some repairs, when she asked me if I would like a cup of coffee. I replied, 'Yes please'. Then she came up to me with, not a cup, but a mug, the very same mug that Angela has, the one she saw in her nightmare'. Christopher thought that this was too much of a coincidence. 'Why, out of all the mugs made in England and moreover all the different types of Jubilee mugs made, was this one offered to me with coffee in it?' I must admit I did find this spooky, we ourselves had at least six Jubilee mugs, all different in design and colouring.

The next day, Gordon's mother rang to thank me for enquiring about her son. Apparently he was fine, the only thing that did bother her about Gordon being in Scotland was that the evening news had mentioned a small earth-quake there!

Since this episode, I have tried really hard not to involve my children in sharing my inner feelings.

This is one of those scenarios which I experience but am unable to do anything about; sometimes because I do not know exactly where the incident is happening.

CHAPTER 18

Dianne's First Extra-Terrestrial Healing

M y wife Dianne suffers from all sorts of ailments, my Orion friends must have 'adopted' her, because they certainly have helped cure some of her ills.

Dianne said that during her childhood years she constantly suffered from lower back pain and 'tummy ache'. Since she hated infant school Dianne said she faked many illnesses so that her mother would keep her off school. Subsequently when she really was poorly with backache and constant visits to the toilet, her mother was reluctant to believe her. My wife said that she could remember when she was six years old being asked by a doctor to bend over so he could test her back, well she laughed and that did it, Dianne wasn't taken very seriously after that. Diane told me that the pain became part of her life and she learned to live with it.

Several years into our marriage Dianne started to develop more serious problems. During the pregnancy of our second baby she was in constant pain. The doctor did not pick up on anything specific, other than the weight of the baby pushing on Dianne's bladder, and diagnosed stress as the cause. Three-quarters of the way through the pregnancy we moved house. With all the upheaval, combined with Dianne moving things about, she was in agony by the time we had moved into our new home.

Dianne thought she was in early labour because she was passing blood and had lower back pain. Now, as luck would have it, a doctor lived right next door. Since we had only been in the house a few hours, I felt I was being rather intrusive when I asked him to see Dianne. Fortunately the doctor instantly recognised that the pain was coming from Dianne's kidneys. He settled her down and gave her a course of medication, and then continued to keep a close eye on her for the rest of her pregnancy.

Time went on and a third child was born without too much trouble, although the water problem was a nuisance. A short while after this birth, however, Dianne started getting almost non-stop kidney infections and was in a great deal of discomfort. The Doctor sent her to hospital for an X-ray and an intravenous pylagram: this is where a dye is passed through the body so the workings can be monitored.

Dianne said that while the procedure was taking place she could see that the doctors looked rather disturbed and were talking, but would not share their findings with her. After it was over, all they said was, 'Make sure you get an appointment to get the results from your consultant'. She made the appointment and duly went along.

'Mrs. Walters', the consultant said, 'you will be pleased to know that there is no disease of your kidneys, but what we have discovered is that you have three of them. You have two kidneys on one side, these are not working correctly. The top half of one kidney functions properly as does the bottom half of the other one. There are two sets of tubing both pumping urine down towards the bladder, but as they are tangled, sometimes this tubing pumps the urine back up. This is why you get infections and pain - you are storing stale urine'. He advised Dianne that arrangements would be made fairly soon for her to be admitted to hospital for an operation. In order to remove the tangle, some bits needed to be taken away leaving one set to do the job.

An appointment came through for Dianne to have a small exploratory operation performed, to ascertain whether or not she had two uteruses. The time quickly came round for her to have this done. Since the procedure was a day surgery, Dianne returned home fairly quickly and was told that she would be advised of the outcome, and given a further appointment for the more serious surgery.

Time passed, we still hadn't heard anything, and Dianne

was in a great deal of pain. It was difficult enough for her coping with three young children as it was. Dianne even found it too painful to drive. As a passenger she sat with a cushion in her back.

During this period of my life I was just coming to terms with what was happening to me. I knew that the Orions, my tall blonde friends, who I now considered almost family, were with me. I asked them to help Dianne. As the weeks passed, there was a marked improvement in her, she stopped moaning and groaning and was driving her car again with ease. I was assuming that she had indeed been helped. I didn't tell Dianne about this until years after. I was really just starting to understand and cope with the contacts myself and trying to deal with the implications of what it all might mean.

The strange and interesting thing about this episode with Dianne's kidneys is, that she has not had any further trouble with them since. Even stranger, Dianne never received any hospital appointment to have the operation, which the doctors were regarding as serious. In fact, it was never mentioned ever again. You would have thought at least someone would have mentioned it on the routine or non-urgent occasions that Dianne has visited the Doctors since! It was as though all the details pertaining to the findings had been eradicated from everyone's mind - perhaps this was the reason: my Orion friends had helped.

Dianne's Second Extra-Terrestrial Healing

T he second time I asked my Orion friends to help Dianne began in May 1989. We had decided to visit Hampton Court Palace for the day with our friend Gordon and his partner. After having parked the car we walked towards the Palace. The roads were very busy so we decided, along with everyone else, to risk crossing to the middle of the carriageway before contemplating traversing the other half. Whilst waiting in the middle of the carriageway, Gordon said 'Okay - go', but the road was not clear. Dianne stupidly crossed the road without looking and a fast moving bicycle collided with her. The bike and male rider landed on top of her. Poor Dianne was bruised all over.

Dianne complained mostly about her knee. She could not walk properly and as a result we had to abandon our day and go home. The next day Dianne's knee was quite a size and very stiff. She limped about for a day or two then decided that perhaps she should see a doctor, as she could not bend it. In fact Dianne was marching about as if she had a wooden leg. She did see a doctor, who referred her for an X-ray, but this showed no broken bones, just swelling.

Well, the knee didn't improve. Once again she couldn't drive, or generally get about, let alone get into a bath or simply sit down. Dianne's leg would not bend. Getting very frustrated she returned to the doctor to see what help might be available. The doctor said he would refer her to a specialist but that it might take a while for her to get an appointment - perhaps as long as six weeks.

Dianne was very upset, a week passed, and she told me that she couldn't carry on any longer like this. She said, 'I'm going to ring the surgery and see if the doctors can get me an earlier appointment'. The doctor's reply was, 'No', because he regarded her case as non-urgent. Looking at Dianne's dilemma, I asked the Orions for help.

Help came during the following evening. I was just relaxing in bed, when my 'friends' came, it was like they were at a party - they were talking non-stop to me. I said out loud, so Dianne could hear, 'If I'm going to put up with your constant noise and chatter tonight, I will listen provided you put Dianne's knee right'. I leaned over at this point and put my head on her bad knee.

The morning came. Dianne always rises first and she went down the nearest small flight of stairs, we have a half galleried landing. She was just about to go down the second flight when she shouted to me, 'Terry look, I can bend my knee'. She started swinging it to and fro. 'It's okay; it got better as if by magic!'

To this day all has been well with the knee. Once again no appointment was ever received and no one ever mentioned it again.

Chapter 20

Healing Through Spiritual Thought

W ithout trying to sound 'Godly', I never ceased to be amazed by perfect strangers coming up to me and asking if I can help them with their illnesses. How do they know what happens to me? So many people when they first see me say, 'Where do I know you from?' Some acquaintances who have never heard me speak about my life, just seem to ring up for no particular reason other than idle chat.

When I ask if there is any particular reason for their telephone calls. They say that they get strength, inspiration, or some sort of energy or power from me, which enables them to cope with their busy day to day lives. One chap was actually dying from cancer. I told him I could not help him to get well, but he replied, 'I know, but you do not know how well I feel for a few weeks after speaking with you'.

In 1991 a family relative was pregnant, she was told that her unborn baby was going to be born with a stomach defect. Apparently her stomach was on the outside of her body. When the little baby girl was born she underwent a lot of surgery and was seriously ill. Three times she stopped breathing, it was a very anxious period over several months before she was out of danger. The particular family did not know too much about me. I thought so much about this little baby, willing her well, although I never actually went to see her.

During the spring of 1996 something a little strange and unexpected happened. I was at my mother's house when this very same little girl came up to me and laid herself affectionately across my lap. This was very out of character. I knew she liked me, but she had always been a little reserved. I must say I was quite 'taken aback' by her mood this partic-

136

ular day. She came close to my face and asked, 'Who are you?' I said, 'Uncle Terry'. She replied 'Uncle Terry I've seen an Angel'. I said 'How lovely, was it nice?' She replied 'Oh yes'. I couldn't help feeling that she might have had an experience, when she was very ill as a tiny baby. She didn't say anything else, but climbed down off my lap and ran away to play.

CHAPTER 21

The Incredible Healing of Louise

J ust to remind you, all the stories in this book are non-fictional. With this in mind and for the want of better words, I would like to tell you of a message I received one day. Some people relate to voices in their heads, I don't. I believe my experiences are very powerful and unique to me.

I'll begin by telling you about an accident that happened to a young girl, Louise, in my neighbouring village. This turned out to be another event to have quite an impact in my life. All incidents are of importance, but when children are involved this is especially true. With Louise, I experienced a vision in connection with her, two weeks prior to her accident.

This is what happened:

In the early hours of a November morning in 1989 I sat up in bed, it was about 5 a.m. I had a vision of names and places, it was very vivid. I asked Dianne if there was any paper in the bedroom to write on. She looked around and brought me a clean piece of white cardboard. Immediately I started to write everything down that I was sensing. I wrote: *Mummy Loony, Loo Loo* (which later I realised was supposed to be *Lu-Lu*), *Foreign Man* and *Ten Beds*. I drew a picture of an entrance to the inside of a building which included a desk and a staircase. I also drew a large room with glass partitioning, which seemed difficult to get into. I spoke about it for a little while to Dianne and then we went back to sleep.

A couple of weeks passed. I was reading the local news-paper when I saw the story of a young girl, Louise, who had been run over by a car. It was terrible, the forecast for her was grim. The accident did not set off any bells ringing at first, but a week later in the paper, the news said Louise was critical, she was losing her fight to live. It was reported that the doctors gave her a less than fifty-fifty chance of survival. My wife said, 'Just look at her photo, she looks so lovely, isn't there anything you can do for her?' I somehow had a feeling that I should.

The newspaper did not print Louise's exact address, only the road turning and the housing estate it was on. I decided to drive to the turning. I went up to the end of it and just before I reached the bottom, I knew where Louise lived. Immediately I went and knocked on the door. Louise's neighbour was in the house and she answered the door at first, then she got the mother. I said to her, 'I hope you do not mind me coming around. I've read about your daughter in the paper. I'm not a 'weirdo' but it seems that whenever I'm around children that are ill, they seem to get better or benefit from my being there'. I told her that I would go home but would leave my telephone number in case she wanted to contact me. She obviously would need to think about it and consult with her husband.

As I reached home and was parking the car I heard my telephone ringing. I rushed into the house to answer it. It was Louise's father calling. He said that he had listened to his wife Sheelagh, and found that what I had to say gave them hope. Louise's father said that they were desperate and asked if I could come back to their home and see them. He then asked how much this was going to cost, I replied 'I do not charge'.

It took me ten minutes to return to their home. When I arrived I introduced myself properly. I said that it was important for me to go into Louise's bedroom. Sheelagh said 'No, you can't do that!' Louise's dad, Tony, told me that this was the room where they took off Louise's blood stained clothes. The room had not been touched or entered since. However I felt that I must go in. Tony agreed and we both went in together. Once inside I started to pick up information. I could hear Louise speaking, and I had a great feeling that maybe I could now be of some help to the family. I asked Sheelagh and Tony for a photo of Louise, which they gave to me. I put it in the breast pocket of my shirt facing outwards. Apparently, Sheelagh told me at a later time that she had seen this photo turn around in my pocket to face inward towards my heart. She was certainly amazed at what she had witnessed. Soon afterwards I left the house saying that I would be available if they wanted me to see Louise in hospital.

As I was driving home a very strange thing happened - the photo in my pocket had turned around again so that Louise's face was facing outwards, instead of inward towards my body! I said 'Oh, sorry Louise.' I reached home and told my wife what had happened.

A short while passed when I received another phone call from Tony. He asked if I could go to the hospital straight away. I was very pleased that they had felt comfortable enough with me, to ask this. We arranged to meet at a local garage where we would fill our cars up with petrol prior to the journey to the Oxford Radcliffe Infirmary where Louise was in intensive care.

At the garage I went up to Tony and confronted him outright and said, 'Tony, you are not Louise's father are you?' He looked at me with a puzzled expression and said, 'No I'm not, how do you know that?' I told him that this was one of the things I had picked up from Louise whilst in her bedroom. I told Tony that Louise called him by his first name and not the usual 'Daddy'. We agreed that we would not mention this to anyone else.

I was anxious to get on with the journey now, I looked into their car at the whole family, Louise had younger twin sisters. They all looked so terribly sad. It took just over an hour to reach the hospital. We parked up and reached the reception area. I looked around and it was just like the pictures I had drawn. The desk and staircase were just the same. I didn't say anything at this point to the family. As we approached the Intensive Care Unit I realised my illustrations were again correct; there was a lot of glass partitioning and it was awkward to find the way in. There were ten beds in the unit, exactly the amount I had drawn. In one bed, there was a foreign man, I had also made a note of this. Before I reached Louise, I passed a young woman who was just being given the 'last rites' by a priest, she looked dreadful. Her head was almost twice the size it should be, apparently due to a road traffic accident; a bus had hit a wall and the wall had fallen on her. However I knew she was going to survive - she said 'Hello' to me - obviously through my mind.

At last we came across Louise, looking white and frail, all wired up and on a life support machine. I sat next to her and held her hand. Then so much started to happen, I knew my 'friends' were around, I felt their presence. I told Sheelagh to talk to Louise, I said that she could hear her. Sheelagh wanted to believe me, but I felt somehow that she thought it was too good to be true and I knew she needed some convincing. I said to her, 'Louise wants her new nightclothes, the blue ones with multicoloured balloons on'. Sheelagh looked back at me, smiled and said, 'Terry, no one knows about them, I've hardly seen them, someone brought them round to the house as a present for her'. I replied, 'She hates that white gown they have put her in'. Sheelagh bent over Louise and cuddled her and told her how much she loved her. For the first time since her accident Louise made a response, tears trickled down her cheeks. Sheelagh cried with joy, it was very emotional and a huge break-through. I was so relieved, but had every confidence in my Orion friends; if they are involved they never let me down.

We phoned Tony and got him to bring the new nightclothes in. I stayed for a little while and then left saying that I would return the next day if they wished. We agreed to do this and arranged to meet at the same time the following day.

Louise's accident was quite a big story in the local town, everyone was very sad. I telephoned my friend Isabel, who was the Borough Mayor at the time. I asked her if she would come with Dianne and me to visit the hospital, subject to Louise's family agreeing.

I wanted Isabel involved as much as possible, as I needed her help and support to campaign about better safety measures for the road where Louise was knocked down. Three children had already died near to the same spot. We were all given permission to visit Louise and we met that afternoon. I, like everyone else, wanted to see how she was progressing. The hospital staff all seemed elated with Louise's changed condition. I sat near to Louise and told her mother what she was telling me, that Louise felt she was without her legs and that she might be disfigured. I spoke out loud for everyone to hear, rather than communicate telepathically with Louise. I announced that in a few moments a nurse would enter, do a small test on Louise - and this was to let her know that she still had her legs. I told Louise that she was not disfigured in any way, I said she looked lovely. Just as I was speaking a nurse came up to Louise with a little bowl and said, 'Louise I'm just going to prick your feet so you can feel them, so that you will know you still have your legs and feet'. Everyone stared at me. Isabel was not surprised at this revelation as she has witnessed similar things with me. However I felt this did help to reassure Louise's mother.

Sheelagh by now was a changed person. She had been in Louise's bedroom and tidied it all up and was thinking positively. As with the previous day I only stayed a short while and left the family alone. On the way out of Intensive Care, the Hospital Chaplain came up to me and asked, 'Who are you?' I replied, by just saying that people seem to get well when I'm around. He responded, 'Well they certainly are all getting well in this Intensive Care Unit, can you come here on a regular basis?' 'Probably not', I replied. However, I did tell him and Louise's family that the young lady who had been so badly injured by a falling wall would be up and helping out on the wards in a couple of months. The Chaplain said she was getting better and that before I came, she was on the brink of death.

It was the next day I believe, that Sheelagh rang to tell me that the hospital had taken Louise off the life support machine, she was really thrilled. However this did not last long, Louise had to be put back on it. The day after this, the hospital said they were sending Louise for another brain scan. Sheelagh was distraught. She phoned her husband, Tony who was at work and she phoned me. I rushed to the hospital and comforted her. I said, 'Stop panicking. They have taken her off the machine too quickly, she needed a little more help. The rapid improvement may have affected their judgement'. Louise was already having her scan, so I took Sheelagh to the canteen for a cup of tea. I said to her that when we returned to the ward Louise would be back in bed, and that her scan would be fine. Sheelagh thought that she might have a slight disability. I told her that when Louise was perfectly well, she would be much cleverer and stronger than ever before. Sheelagh 'cried her eyes out' and told me all about her own childhood and life up to date. She got a lot off her chest and it did her a lot of good.

We returned to the ward and there indeed was Louise back in her bed, the scan result was fine. The doctor said, 'We think we took her off the machine a bit too quickly, we will do it more gradually, over the next couple of days'. Sheelagh sighed with relief and I left her again as I knew that Tony was already on his way up to her.

We kept in telephone contact over the next few weeks. I didn't feel the need to go there anymore. I soon received the telephone call that Louise was coming home for Christmas, and I was invited around with my wife to see her. Louise was almost better apart from a bit of confusion, but did draw a nice picture for me and wrote on it, 'From Lu Lu'.

A short while passed before Louise was home for good.

One day I asked Sheelagh if we all could go to a local bird sanctuary and have a walk around, there was quite a lot to do there. I felt the stimulation would be good for Louise. I then told Sheelagh that I could see that a small bone in Louise's head was still cracked, it was behind her ear region and I recommended that it should be treated at some time in the near future. I felt that the hospital had probably missed it. Sheelagh listened.

Louise returned to school and worked hard at catching up. I kept in contact with the family on a low key basis. I felt that if they needed me further they would call. A couple of months had passed when I drew more things in the early hours of the morning. I drew a little white cupboard with a door that wouldn't shut and the face of a Chinese man, I wrote next to it 'Chang'. In the morning I received a telephone call, it was Sheelagh in sheer panic. 'Terry please go to the local hospital, Louise has been taken there, she is very ill with meningitis'. I told her that I would leave straight away.

When I reached the hospital, I made my way to the Children's Unit. I spotted Louise in a side ward, she opened her eyes and looked at me. I said to her, 'Come on Lu, stop giving us these scares'. She smiled. I sat with her, then I noticed she had a bedside cabinet in the room just like the one I had drawn, it had the door hanging awkwardly and it wouldn't shut. Sheelagh came in and sat with us, she told me that Louise didn't like her doctor, she said 'He is Chinese'. I looked above her bed, there it said 'Dr. Chang'. So once again this was no coincidence, I was needed and so were my Orion friends.

I told Sheelagh about my drawings and I tried to tell her not to worry. I said the illness was due to the cracked bone behind Louise's ear, which I had described to her earlier, and that when she was well we should really take her back to the Oxford Radcliffe Infirmary for treatment. The next day I rang Sheelagh for an update, Louise was supposed to be undergoing treatment for the meningitis. I visited the hospital, but Louise wasn't in her bed. I was about to go and look for her, when a nurse came up to me and said, 'I saw you looking and talking to Louise yesterday. She responded when she was in contact with you'.

I strolled down to the day room and spotted Louise playing a guessing game with another girl patient. I thought I would test something out. I actually put thoughts in Louise's head, regarding the game she was playing, it worked. Louise was saying exactly what I was thinking. I knew she was definitely being helped and guided, and healed through me by my 'friends'. Louise and her family seemed quite happy with the situation, so I went home.

Louise did return to the Oxford hospital and get herself sorted out. The family carried on with life and Louise got on very well at school. We stayed in touch from time to time, it was very encouraging to hear of Louise's great progress, she went on to do her 'A' levels.

I was told that the family would soon be moving, but Louise did not want to go. Apparently Louise did not leave immediately, but stayed with a family for a while whilst she did her exams; but it didn't work out and so she joined her mum and sisters in the North of England. However before she went she called on me a couple of times. Louise wanted to ask me about the time she was ill. She said that she could remember my voice, and then she started to tell me about things that were happening to her. At first she thought that she might be ridiculed. Louise said that she hadn't even told her mother what she was about to tell me. I said to her, 'I'll never ridicule you, just tell me'. Louise went on to say that since her recovery she has started to predict and to see things happen before they 'come to light'. But, from my point of view, the most revealing thing she said, was that she wanted to be up in the sky. Apparently Louise had an overwhelming feeling of wanting to be with 'sky people'. I don't think she really understood why, and she looked to me for answers. I told her a little bit of what happens to me, but I didn't want to fill her head with my life. After I spoke to her she seemed less confused, but was obviously keen to know more. I suggested that she might ask her mother, as Sheelagh was a witness to the strange events that took place during Louise's recovery.

It turned out that Louise, because of her love for the sky, wanted to pursue a career as a pilot. She bought some books and did some studying; but she was very disappointed to find out that because she'd had brain surgery she would never be allowed to fly solo.

I recently spoke to Louise and her Mum (August 1996) and she has certainly faired well. Louise passed all her 'A' levels and is doing Advanced Business Studies. She has also been nominated for a City and Guilds Award of Excellence.

VERIFICATION

'The first time I met Terry was not long after Lu had her accident and was in a coma. After finding my address, Terry came to my house claiming that he was not a faith-healer, but would be able to help me. I was a little dubious at first, but I had nothing to lose, so I let him in.

'Terry then asked to see Lu's bedroom. I wanted to say 'No' because it was a sacred place for me and I would not let anyone inside it. After a lot of thought, I let him see the room. After which, he asked me for a photo of Lu. He placed this photo in his pocket on the left hand side of his shirt. The shirt had a blue and white striped pattern. It was made of thin cotton, because the pocket was more or less see-through, I could see the photo facing outwards towards me.

'We then went down the stairs and Terry had his hands in his trouser pockets at all times. I remember this because I was still

Crash girl goes home

Louise Williams pictured before her accident

ROAD crash victim Louise Williams has returned home to her family — defying doctors who weeks ago gave her a less than 50/50 chance of survival.

But sadly part of Louise's memory was wiped in the horrific accident and she cannot even recognise every day objects.

Now her father David Logan and mother Shellagh are patiently teaching their daughter, who was in a coma for two weeks, the basic lessons of life.

The 11-year-old also still has to undergo tests to assess if she has suffered any lasting brain damage from the accident.

Mr Logan said yesterday: "We are very pleased that she has come home. She is walking and talking but she keeps calling things by the wrong name.

"She is going for an assessment at the hospital tomorrow when we will know if there is any permanent damage."

Louise was in collision with a car on November 28 as she was crossing South

By MARK PALIN

Hill Road at the junction with Reeds Hill, near a playground where she had been playing.

Louise lay in a coma in Oxford's Radcliffe Infirmary, which specalises in severe head injuries, as doctors were too afraid to operate for fear of endangering her life.

After treatment, she was transferred to Wexham Park Hospital in Slough to complete her amazing recovery.

Her parents kept a constant vigil praying for the day when they would be able to take her home.

Mr Logan said: "On Christmas Day she came home for a couple of hours but we then had to take her back to hospital.

"There have been lots of little presents from people and friends and she has now opened them all. A few of her friends have come around to see her."

Louise had started her first year at Brakenhale School a few weeks before the accident on the jinxed junction.

Three children have died on the junction since 1975, the latest in January 1988.

Bracknell town council will discuss the fencing around the playground on the junction, opposite the Golden Farmer pub, next Tuesday.

Easthampstead borough councillor Isabel Mattick has proposed putting a pelican crossing outside the pub to help reduce the risk of accidents.

But Mr Logan said the idea was "daft," adding: "By the time motorists turn the corner they will be on top of it.

"I have seen cars go through the pelican crossing on that road even when the lights are on red."

The playground on South Hill Road, Bracknell ©

suspicious about him and kept my eyes on him. He then said 'Louise has turned over!' With this, I looked at his shirt and the photo was now facing towards his heart and I knew that he had not moved it. This incident scared me a little and made me realize that Terry was genuine and may be able to help after all.

GNVQ PROGRESS

Congratulations to all those students whose work was externally verified in June where a good standard of work was confirmed. Special congratulations to Louise Williams of 13JT whose work so impressed the External Verifier that he recommended her for entry to the City and Guilds Medal for Excellence Award on completion of Advanced Level Business GNVQ.

Inermediate GNVQ students are almost at the end of their course having survived a hectic schedule of assignments and unit tests. Advanced level students in Business and Health and Social Care continue their progress with many working through the summer on individual assignments and planning their applications to university.

Many Intermediate Business Students are progressing to the Advanced level next year and we look forward to welcoming them back. To those who are leaving for employment or further education we wish you success, secure in the knowledge that GNVQ has given you a head start. We are proud of your achievements.

CAROL FITZGERALD
AND THE GNVQ
TEAM

'The next incident which happened was not long after the first, while Lu was still in a coma. At this stage, Terry had still not seen Lu. Her godmother had gone to see her to give her some new night clothes, but because I hadn't visited her yet that day, I did not know what they looked like. That same day, Terry came around saying that he had a picture of her in his mind and she was surrounded by balloons, but could not understand why. Later on, I visited Lu and there, placed on top of her were the new night clothes patterned with balloons. This then explained Terry's picture.

'After Lu had recovered from her accident, she suffered from meningitis twice. One thing I never told anyone, not even Lu, was the fact that she suffered from this illness when she was a baby as well. I never told Terry this, but somehow he knew.'

By Lu
'When I was in hospital with meningitis Terry visited me. But before he did, Terry drew a picture of a hospital bedside cabinet with a door which would not close. When he came to see me, we found that his picture was identical to my cabinet. Later, he drew a picture of a Chinese doctor, before he had seen my doctor. Out of all of the different origins of doctors available, I had a Chinese one.'

CHAPTER 22

Extra-Terrestrial Help in Understanding Julie's Sickness.

I suppose I must say that my family and friends are probably the first to benefit a lot from the healing that comes through me.

Approximately five years ago my eldest daughter Julie was very unwell, she was suffering severe pain in her lower abdomen and side, and being sick. A doctor was called and he thought it was appendicitis. The doctor said that Julie was to call him if it got worse.

Julie made attempts all day to contact my wife and I, but we were out. We didn't get her call until the evening. Julie's husband telephoned and said that she was rolling around in pain on her bed, but that he did not want to do anything until we went round. When I got there Julie was in a bad state. I rang for an ambulance, but they wouldn't come out because a doctor hadn't referred the case. I decided to put Julie in my car and drive her to the hospital myself, rather than wait for the doctor to return and then wait for him to consider the situation and get an ambulance.

I had to stop several times on the way to the hospital for Julie to be sick. When we finally reached there, she was seen by doctors who agreed that she probably did have appendicitis. She was put into a bed. The staff had to ring round for an anaesthetist to come to the hospital, it was quite late by now, around eleven p.m.

The doctors said that Julie needed an emergency operation. I made the fatal mistake, I said to Julie, 'You haven't got anything wrong with your appendix'. Well, that did it. Julie would not sign the operation consent form. The hospital staff were not at all pleased. I said to Julie that she could not carry on the way she was, and I didn't know myself what should happen. My wife and I left the hospital, leaving Julie in their hands. I was hoping they would re-examine her and find something else.

We had a dreadful night worrying about Julie. I asked my Orion friends what was wrong with her, they said that it wasn't her appendix. So what was it? They showed me a small oblong object, it was purple with small circles inside it. They used the word 'compound'. I racked my brains as to what it might be. I asked Dianne, she said that she could not think of anything, so I asked my 'friends' again for more information. They said that we had touched it that evening at Julie's place. They were so cryptic it was very annoying. Dianne said that if we had touched it, it must have been something in Julie's kitchen that had made her ill. As we were getting Julie ready to go to the hospital, we had moved things around in her kitchen, looking for her brush and comb and some things to take with us to the hospital. Dianne asked me to draw what I was being shown.

Dianne remarked, 'That's her contraceptive pill packet'. We had touched it, we put it on a shelf.

It was soon early morning, the telephone rang, it was Julie from the hospital. She had suffered all night and had not allowed the doctors to touch her, she was crying and said that they needed to operate and that she must allow them to proceed. I said to Julie 'Let them do it', and I said that we would leave straight away to be with her. I made a quick phone call to my Reverend friend, Robert Beatty, whose wife was a surgeon. I explained what had happened and he said to me, 'Yes, let them go ahead, even if you are being told that it is the pill that is making her ill, go with her and look after her, she should be fine, we can live without our appendix'.

One odd thing Robert did say to me was, that we should always go to a reputable dispensing chemist. He recommended one, because he said that some places issue inferior 'compounds'. Robert used the word the Orion's had said to me, and I had not mentioned this word to Robert before hand.

Julie was just going into the operating theatre when we arrived at the hospital. I held Julie's hand and said that Mum and I would be waiting for her to come out. The operation was performed and we stayed with Julie for some time. During that period a doctor came up to us and said, 'We have just taken out a perfectly good appendix'.

Julie was hopping mad, I told her to calm down and explained what had happened to me during the night, and what Robert had said. Julie then said, 'God, yes, it's since I've been taking that brand of birth control pill, I've been getting unwell'. It obviously didn't agree with her.

Very soon Julie was up and about and returned home. Strangely enough, to this day, five years on or so, Julie has never taken another contraceptive pill, which was her only method of birth control, and she has not become pregnant again. It appears that she has her own protection now, without having to take any pill. If she ever wanted more children, I will have to ask my 'friends' for a reversal.

CHAPTER 23

UFO Sightings

E arly one evening during the winter of 1994, I was driving to my mother's home, which was only ten minutes away from where I lived. The most direct route to her house was via a winding country road, about four miles long. I had gone only a couple of miles when I was startled by a large blue light appearing from a field to the left of me, it crossed over the lane into a field to the right. All of a sudden, it materialised into a spacecraft. At that moment it came across the top of my car and hovered. I felt extremely uneasy and all sorts of things went through my mind.

My first thought was to veer into a lay-by and grab my mobile phone. As soon as I touched it, the phone started dialling by itself reaching a neighbour who spoke to me. I was astonished and said, 'I didn't ring you'. I hurriedly tried to explain what was happening, but then decided to press the 'end' button, as I urgently wanted to speak to Dianne just in case the UFO caused me to disappear. But before I could ring her, the mobile phone automatically dialled another one of my neighbours. It was bizarre. I did manage to contact Dianne eventually, but only very briefly, because the phone was acting so erratically. So I decided to pull the battery off. The phone kept on dialling! How could this be? Then as quickly as the craft came, it went.

My next thought was to get away and drive somewhere where it was light, but before I left the lay-by, a car pulled in behind me. This made me all the more nervous and determined to get away quickly and I proceeded to drive to a local garage. The car behind followed me all the way to the garage, and it wasn't until I got under the forecourt lights that I realised it was Mark's car, a friend of mine. I didn't have wait long to find out what he was doing, because he jumped out of his car and rushed over to me to explain, even before I had a chance to tell him what I had just seen.

Mark said that he had been travelling home on the M4 motorway, which is near to the country lane I was driving along, when he saw in the sky to the right of him a large blue light, which took the form of a UFO, at least, that's what he thought. Mark was completely 'taken aback' and over-whelmed by this sighting but he couldn't quite believe what he was seeing, or be sure of what the object was.

He then said he had to make a split decision, either to come off at the next exit on the motorway and come directly round to my house (Mark knew of my involvement with UFOs) and tell me about what he had seen, or go straight home. He made his way to me. After driving only halfway down the same lane that I was on, Mark was shocked at seeing my car in the lay-by. Puzzled at meeting me like that, he followed me to the garage. Mark's description of the object and light were the same as mine and I felt that I was not alone in this sighting.

We spoke for a while and arranged to meet the next day. I carried on to my mother's home and then returned home to explain to Dianne what had happened. When I got back, I found a number of neighbours on their doorsteps looking at the sky! The UFO had long gone though.

That evening, before I went to bed, I put the battery of my phone on charge as usual, but in the morning when I put it back on I discovered that it had not recharged, it was completely dead. I was annoyed as the mobile phone was fairly new. I tried recharging it again, but it was useless.

I have heard of UFOs interfering with car electric's but until I see proof for myself I tend to keep an open mind. Well, proof I had! My car had developed an electrical problem. The following day the car was barely running. It was very lumpy as the engine turned over and it kept cutting out. However, I thought it might correct itself because it ran okay. for some of the time.

I therefore decided to risk taking it on a long journey to the south coast at the weekend, but I did put the jump leads in the car just in case I needed them. I was taking my wife, son-in-law and his mother to see my friend Reg Presley from the 1960's Rock n' Roll Band, 'The Troggs', who were taking part in a sixties revival show.

Apart from several small juddering vibrations in the car we arrived at the show alright, even though I thought at one time the engine might 'cut out'. The show was brilliant, 'The Troggs' were the last band to play, so they didn't finish until about 2 a.m. Afterwards, we all went to the dressing room and chatted to them for about forty-five minutes. It was well into the early hours of the morning before we started for home.

The car behaved itself until we were three-quarters of the way back, but then it just slowly stopped. I managed to pull slightly off the road, got out and looked under the bonnet to see if I could see the problem. If so, perhaps I could restart it, but it looked all right. I didn't smell any burning and I asked my son-in-law to turn the engine over but nothing happened. We looked at each other and thought, well that's it, we're stuck.

My mobile phone was useless, by now I realized the battery had completely 'had it' and I couldn't phone anyone. I thought I would have to walk to a call box, to get help so I shut the bonnet down, but as I did this the car started! Without even wondering why, I dashed back into the car and drove home. The next day the car would not start. I called an automotive electrical engineer to look at it as I was busy. He said he didn't know how I had been driving it because the wiring was all burned out. Not only did I have to buy a new battery for my phone, but I also decided to purchase a new car!

CHAPTER 24

Warning of Danger

A great deal of my life has been about providing important messages, messages that have been given to me to
warn people of impending danger. One such story involved
my granddaughter.

Around 5 a.m. one morning I woke my wife and said,
'What time does Julie (my eldest daughter) take Barry to
school'. (Barry is my eldest grandchild). Dianne said 'She
leaves home about 8.45 a.m'. I told Dianne not to let me
oversleep because I had to go to Julie's home and warn her
of something I had seen. I could not telephone her because
at the time she was not connected. Dianne by now, was too
frightened to go back to sleep in case we both overslept, so
she stayed awake.

I drove to Julie's house and arrived at 8.30 a.m. She was
with a neighbour, they walked the children to school
together. I told Julie what I had seen: It was definitely real;
my youngest granddaughter, Rebecca, was being taken away
by a man, from a little copse of woods near to the bottom
of her garden. I asked Julie if she left Rebecca alone at all,
perhaps outside a shop en-route to school, or maybe Barry
would accidentally leave the back garden gate open, for her
to wander off into the wood? Julie reassured me that she
would not let her out of her sight, so off they went to the
local school, along with a bewildered neighbour.

At 3.15 p.m. that afternoon Julie rang me from a telephone box near to the school, 'Dad!' she screamed, 'Guess
what? The school is swarming with police, a little girl was
taken away from that wooded area you said about'.

Thankfully the little girl was returned a couple of hours
later to a local shopping parade, with a coin in her hand.
The incident was shown on the television that evening and

of course featured in the local papers. Julie's neighbour was surprised by the whole thing, and must have thought me very strange.

CHAPTER 25

Healing through Distance

Whatever this healing power is I seem to have, it works in different forms. Like other healers, I do not necessarily have to be with people for it to work. Just by speaking with them over the telephone or by seeing a picture or photograph of them, or just by mind only, various forms of healing take place.

I think the story I am about to tell, about a gentleman from Illinois, USA, is probably the farthest distance over which I've ever been asked to help, not particularly to heal him but to put his life together, a life which had been in disarray.

It all started on 26th May 1991. My daughter Angela now at work for a company in Wokingham in Berkshire, received a fax from a Mr. Richi Franzen. The fax was not meant for Angela at all, it wasn't meant for England either. It was supposed to have gone to someone internally in America, but for some reason it came through to my daughter in England!

Angela let Richi know of the mistake, and he seemed 'well-chuffed'. She received this faxed message back:

FAX

From: Rich Franzen
Subject: Discovered

Ange,

Yes the T-Bird was supposed to go to someone else....But now I know someone in Wokingham. Where on earth is Wokingham? What are the coordinates in relation to Orland Park? What is the reason you want to be discovered? It may be possible to be discovered if one knew for what?

158

Keep in touch,
Richi from Non-Wokingham.

Angela returned a fax telling Richi about herself to which she received another reply:

FAX

From: Rich Franzen
Subject: Nightlife

Hi Ange,
This is fun, trans. Atlantic communication. I think you are 7 or 8 hours ahead of us here. I think when I start work you are leaving for the day, is that right?

No, I don't expect England to be all cottages. I just like English people. They seemed to be refined and interesting.

Orland Park is in Illinois and a suburb of Chicago. It is about twenty miles from the Indiana border.

I have three children, a son 16 and twin daughters 12. I am divorced.

I am an old fart - 44 years old; but I always seem to date women in their mid-twenties - the only problem I have with that is that they want to get married and have babies. Like you, I don't want this. There's too much I want to do and I don't want to be saddled down with babies now.

Besides working here, I am also an author. I have had one novel published and another about to be published. I now have an agent trying to sell my first novel in Sweden and am trying to get contacts in England and Australia as well. If things work out the way I want I'll have reason to go to Sweden, England and Australia to promote my books - hence why I don't want to be home with babies.

Hope to hear from you soon,
Richi.

A few more Fax's were exchanged then Angela received

one - Subject matter 'Ask your Dad'.

FAX

From: Rich Franzen
Subject: Ask your dad.

Ange,

What an interesting subject. Let me tell you about something that just happened to me last week, it was the strangest thing that ever happened to me.

First let me tell you that I have had many supernatural experiences, my ghost stories as I call them. So I am no stranger to this subject. In fact when I tell people about them they get scared, but basically I am a sceptic when it comes to psychics and mediums etc.

Last week I was in Florida, about 40 miles from Miami in a place called Fort Lauderdale. At a writers conference, in fact it was exactly the same day that the Queen was in Miami.

Anyway - *Clue #1* I have never been to Florida before in my life. No one knew me and I knew no one. I was there to meet with some editors to go over my new book.

Clue #2 All during the meeting I was always meeting and talking with people to meet as many people in the business as possible.

So, this one day I decided to take a break and get away from the crowd for a few minutes of solitude. I went to the other side of the hotel and sat down in a place I'd never been before. There sitting next to me is a man who claims to be a psychic healer, just like your Dad. So there I am, sceptical, not even wanting to talk to anyone. He tells me about his ability and I am almost rude to him telling I don't believe in people like him. So he asks me to tell him about myself and I said you're the psychic you tell me because I'm not going to volunteer any information which he could later retell me and claim to be psychic.

160

Anyway, this guy proceeds to tell me things about myself, many things and very personal things which no one knows about me. It started to shake me up let me tell you. And then he starts to tell me about relatives of mine who are dead.

This is a long story, I told someone about it on the phone and it took two hours. I'll only give you the highlights.

So basically he starts to pinpoint problems in my life and difficulties I have to continue facing and it truly amazed me. Then he tells me the reason why. He claims that there are twelve spirits within me, four of which he identified as these relatives who died. He didn't have time to identify the other eight. He claims that these spirits are trying to protect me and in doing so are preventing me from getting what I want out of life - they think they know what's best for me.

So the bottom line is that he claims that these spirits can be removed through hypnosis and then I will be happier and more successful etc.

Have you ever heard anything like this. I still want to be sceptical but all these things he told me so amazed me and made me wonder how could he know these things - and also he told me that my coming to Florida was to meet him and that's why I sat there when I did.

I am certainly thinking about this. He gave me a list of books to read and I am buying them tonight and reading them.

Let me know what your Father has to say about this.

The thirteen of us,
Richi.

The next fax received was titled GB Book - Richi gave Angela some ideas.

FAX

From: Rich Franzen
Subject: GB Book

Ange,

What sort of tips would you like regarding your Father's book? In this country most non-fiction books are sold before they are written. Basically what he would do in the States is write one sample chapter, list his credentials in a coverletter and write a short synopsis about the book and send this off to publishers. The subject matter is selling here in the States. It's a good topic.

Thirteen Richi's.

Richi must have been thinking about things that Angela had been telling him about me, and thought that maybe I could help him. He sent her a fax asking if I would speak to him on the phone to discuss his problem. I told Angela to tell him that I would listen to him if he telephoned me, but first I was having a few days break in Jersey, he could ring me on my return, and a time and date was arranged.

Another fax arrived.

FAX

From: Rich Franzen
Subject: Seeing

Ange,

This man in Florida, that's what he does, through hypnosis is take them spirits to Jesus. I've started reading the books he recommended and it is amazing how common this is and the experiences I can relate to. This is all so new to me and profound and it is making more sense to me by the day. I would most enjoy talking to your Father, as I am investigating every aspect of this before I proceed but I am beginning to believe that I should proceed. What do I have to lose? That's a loaded question. But I feel if I just ignore this it may nag at me for the rest of my life. I hope I am smart enough not to get involved with cult types or con men. I will be cautious and would like to talk with your Father as I said.

I'll send more later. Trying to keep this short and hopefully get this to you before you leave for the day. It's Friday, drinking day for you.

Richi.

I returned from Jersey which wasn't without paranormal incident. I waited for Richi's telephone call bearing in mind what he had said in the last fax. Sure enough Richi phoned. We spoke in all for about half an hour. I instinctively knew what was wrong with him within minutes of talking to him. He did have 12 spirits within him running his life. I told him to get a pen and paper and write the names down. I was about to tell him their names. I said that we would go through them in order and take them away. As I read the names out he was astounded as to how I knew these people. When we reached the twelfth spirit, I said that she was an Aunt, not a bad person, she was helping him to write his books. I asked Richi if he wanted to keep her, he replied 'No, get rid of all of them'. I spoke to the spirits, they understood and left him alone. Richi thanked me and said that he would be in touch with Angela.

FAX

From: Rich Franzen
Subject: Free

Ange,

How are you. It was certainly nice talking on the phone with you, and you do have an accent. I was very apprehensive before calling much like I felt after talking to this man in Florida but the moment your Father started to speak to me I felt very relaxed. He has such a soothing quality about

163

him and it is easy to tell that he is an extraordinary person.

I cannot begin to tell you how nice it was and how grateful I am to both of you for this. I do feel different very much at peace and free of anxiety. It is also strange that before Saturday all I wanted to do was talk about this and now it doesn't seem necessary. I just want to think about it and don't feel such a strong need to talk about it anymore. I have so many feelings that cannot be described in words but they are all good. I suppose I feel sort of mellowed.

I think your Father should write his book as he has such unique experiences and he should share them with us common folk like myself, let me know how he progresses with it.

Your father told me to send my telephone number. In the book I sent I put two of my cards, you should be getting it by today or tomorrow.

Again thank your father for me, and thank you for freeing me - it is wonderful.

Richi.

CHAPTER 26

Conclusion

It is a difficult task to explain in this small book all the incredible things that have happened to me in my life. Some of the experiences are very personal between me and my Orion friends and cannot be passed on.

Aliens, extra-terrestrials, whatever you want to call them are here. It is about time the truth was listened to. Too much emphasis has been placed on abductions, the little 'Greys' and generally putting immense fear into people. My Orion friends are nothing to do with any of this.

The subject should be discussed on prime time television. Children are being taught in schools about religion, geography, Egypt and how life began. But I know that not all of their instruction is right, and so do many other people, including teachers who I've spoken with. I am at present a School Governor. I've obviously never mentioned my views to the children, but I'm rather pleased that my term as a long serving Governor is coming to an end. Perhaps through this book I can now enter the debate from another angle.

The Egyptian connection with Orion is of great importance. When I say great, I feel the word does not truly capture the real significance of what I am saying: the Pyramids were a working machine for the transportation of the Pharaohs to travel to and from Orion. They could be made to work again!

I have a theory that the 'Ark of the Covenant' is part of this mechanism, possibly the main power source to get the Pyramids working. I believe that it comes from Orion and should go back there. There are several cross references in the Bible which back this theory up. The question needs to be asked, if we found the Ark, how would we get it back? Let me just say - it would be taken care of! It is too complex and therefore somewhat difficult to interpret what I know. I feel that it is of such importance, and yet, because it is so advanced, I can't even write it down. When I can I will!

Perhaps I was part of the beginning, along with the Pharaohs. I say this because of the many different aspects of my life and the paranormal activity that surrounds me. Have I the ability to do Egyptian Magic? I can't find any other explanation. I never know what will happen from day to day in my life. I just hope it is all for the good; so far it has been.

I hope it can be appreciated that all the stories and information in this book can be backed up and corroborated. Many people have been with me when strange things have taken place, and it has had a very big impact on their lives.

One day I know that I will find out exactly who on earth I am!

APPENDIX

Dear Mike,

Further to your letter, I hope you find the following useful:

" Although my own work and research does not involve channelling
or other psychic phenomena, I have to acknowledge that I was
much impressed by Terry Walter's unusual telepathic abilities.
Terry is an honest man with truly remarkable insights, and his
autobiographical book will surely be a valuable and welcome addition to the growing new age consciousness that is the hallmark
of the coming millennium."

Robert G. Bauval

Terry Walters

I have been studying the subject of UFOs and allied phenomena since the early sixties. Over the years I have interviewed numerous UFO witnesses, abductees and people claiming to have psychic and channelling abilities. I therefore consider that I have had some experience in the study of people involved in these activities.

It was in late November 1992, that I received a telephone call from Terry Walters. He wanted to discuss some of the strange events that had happened in his life, I believe that he obtained my number through my association with the 'Flying Sauces Review' magazine.

I listened casually at first and then more intently as Terry Walters described some of his past experiences. I had no way of knowing if his claims were true or just a manifestation, but there was something in the intense tone of his voice that convinced me I should meet Terry face to face and soon! I arranged to meet him at his home near Wokingham the following day, a round trip of over 300 miles.

I duly arrived at Terry Walters home, met his wife Dianne and his pet Alsatian. Terry started the conversation in his unmistakable London accent and within a short time he began to disclose some of the amazing events that have befallen him in recent years.

Terry spoke of his contact with aliens, which in turn has given him access to healing powers, together with a psychic sense that has enabled him to 'see' details of past and future events. He told of his ability to travel in alien craft, while undergoing 'out of the body' experiences. As the meeting progressed, Terry covered a number of the strange happenings that have occurred in his life. Terry's wife, Dianne, nodded approvingly, confirming parts of his story, when she had been present. Finally, our discussion was over and I left for home, intrigued by the enigma of Terry's experiences.

Since that meeting in 1992, I have constantly kept in touch with Terry Walters and his continuing life history.

A number of Terry Walters revelations have resulted in the publication of this book. Through personal knowledge I have been able to establish several of his claimed events. As to the remainder of his experiences, I can only assume that they may well be true.

" INCREDIBLE STORIES. -
CREDIBLE MAN..!

KENNETH A. SEDDINGTON.
UK DIRECTOR - INTERNATIONAL UFO
WORLD CONGRESS.

LT

From: Mrs E. C. M. Ford, M.B.E.

MINISTRY OF DEFENCE
Adastral House, Theobalds Road, LONDON W.C.I X 8RU

Telephone: 01-430 7573

Our reference: P.402799/43/AR9(RAF)
Your reference:

5 September 1980

Dear Sir,

Thank you for your letter in which you ask about Wellington HE 213.

I can confirm that this aircraft, of 431 Squadron, took off at 23.22 hours on the 10th April, 1943 with a crew of five to attack a target at Frankfurt. A distress message was received at 06.08 hours on the 11th April 1943, and the aircraft failed to return to base. Information received later stated that three of the crew members were captured on the 11th April 1943, and a subsequent report was received saying that the body of a fourth member of the crew had been washed ashore on the Island of Jersey. The fifth member of the crew was never found and it was assumed that he had been claimed by the sea. He was Sergeant G. A. Booth who is commemorated on the Runnymede Memorial.

News was received from the International Red Cross that the aircraft had been shot down on the 11th August 1943, and captured German documents show that the aircraft crashed into the sea 4 kilometres west of Jersey.

The three survivors of the crew were Sergeants L. C. Bolke, E. A. Odling and W. E. Bidmead.

Yours sincerely

Edna Ford.

APPENDIX

THE CHANNEL ISLANDS OCCUPATION SOCIETY
GUERNSEY BRANCH

Tel: 0481-37015

PLEASE REPLY TO:-

John D. Goodwin.
'La Capelle de Haut'
Villiaze Rd.
St Andrew.
Guernsey. Channel Is.

20th.January.1983.

Dear Mr Bidmead,
        This is the promised letter following my telephone call to you regarding your forced landing in the sea off St Ouen's Bay, Jersey, on the 11th.April.1943. As it was so close to Christmas when I phoned I felt it best to wait until after the festivities before I wrote with my request for information.

        As I mentioned, I am researching the air war over and around the Ch.Is.,in an attempt to produce an accurate and detailed account of all the air activity which occured, an aspect that has been very neglected in the several histories produced to date. Indeed, the inference from most of these works is that little happened in the way of air attacks etc., an impression which has been proved totally incorrect.

        Having consulted the Royal Air Force Group and Sqdn. Operations Record Books at the Public Records Office at Kew, and corresponded with the M.o.D.(Air), a clear pitcure has emerged revealing constant shipping and aerial reconnaissance operations plus successful attacks on vessels at sea, harbours, radar installations and airfields. R.A.F. Bommber Command aircraft regularly passed over or near the Islands enroute to targets in France and several leaflet drops were carried out.

        Some time ago I wrote to the M.o.D. regarding the loss of your Wellington plus the fate of its crew and as you will see from the attached photocopy reply they informed me that three of you had survived. As you know the body of Sgt.Holden was washed ashore on Jersey on 5th.June (1943) and was buried the following day at Mont a l'Abbe Cemetery, but sadly Sgt.Booth was never seen again. Photographs of Sgt.Holdens funeral exist and should you like copies I will gladly forward same.

        I would be most interested to hear about your last operation and what happened during that fateful night. The German gunners claimed to have shot you down but I see from your letter to the newspaper that was not the case. I realise this all occured a long time ago and that perhaps I am asking a great deal but I assure you that any information will be of tremendous value in my research and serve to further our knowledge of this period in our history.
        Hoping this letter finds you in good health and that you will forgive this intrusion into your privacy.

I am Sir, Yours truly

Goodwin

Archivist.
C.I.O.S. Guernsey.

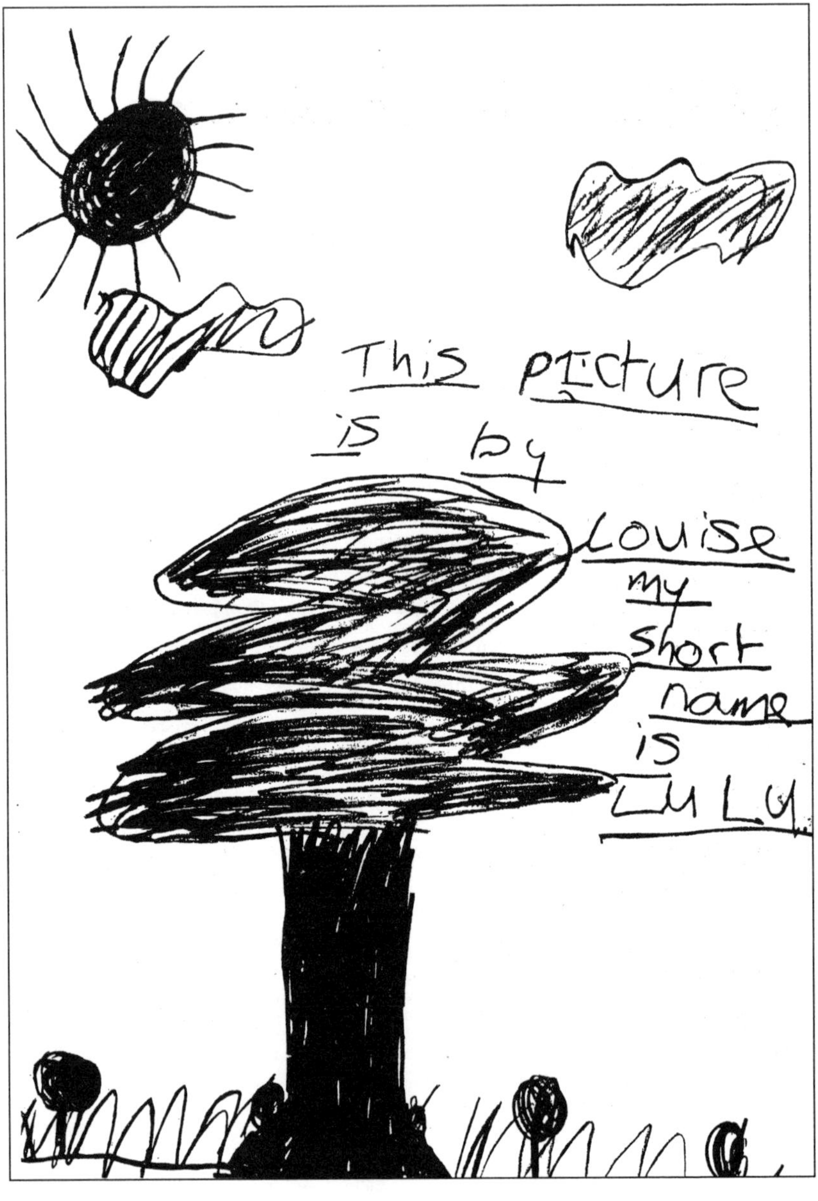
This picture
is by
Louise
my
short
name
is
LULU

NOTES